What people are saying abou

"I've known Elyse Murphy a long way from a pastor's kid woman and communicator, and that honest journey is in this book. Elyse has a passion for helping teenagers—especially those who have grown up in church—make good life decisions, and this book is another powerful resource to help them do just that. I'm so excited for her future and where God is taking her. Here's to the next million years!"

—**Christine Caine, speaker, author, and founder of A21 Campaign**

"Elyse Murphy is one of those remarkable young women who are destined to make a difference in the world! I just love her! In this book, her honesty and genuine love for God will be an inspiration and an encouragement to all who read it."

—**Holly Wagner, Oasis Church, Los Angeles, California,**

founder of GodChicks

"Through *Confessions of a Church Kid*, Elyse brilliantly describes the very real unspoken feelings and challenges that Christians wrestle with. This book is for all ages, giving insight on what the young believer is dealing with while showing the leader and parent how to respond to these confessions. I'm grateful for Elyse's voice to this generation and the message that this book carries—being a church kid myself. I know that this book will bless you."

—**Chris Durso, Misfit NYC, Christ Tabernacle**

"As a pastor's kid, I understand the struggles and pressures that come with such a label. I've known Elyse since she was a little girl— always an infectious smile, cute freckles, and a bright spirit. Her honesty and life experience shared in this book will help not only the children of pastors but pastors raising children, along with anyone leading young people within a church dynamic."

—**Laura Lentz, Hillsong Church, New York City**

"Elyse has wrestled with the tough questions many church kids ask and has found tried and true wisdom and revelation that others can now glean from her life. For myself, being a pastor of a growing church in NYC and the father of four young children, you better believe that they'll be reading this book when the season hits that they need it. I am grateful for Elyse's vulnerability in this book, because my children and many others will inherit her wisdom and be set free."

—**Andi Andrew, lead pastor, Liberty Church, New York City**

"Elyse Murphy's *Confessions of a Church Kid* offers incredible insight on the problems—and more importantly, the solutions—that come from growing up in the church. With her trademark honesty, humor, and strong biblical foundation, Elyse helps readers win the spiritual tug-of-war between knowing God and discovering their place in the world. I heartily recommend this inspiring resource for anyone who wants to grow closer to Jesus."

—**Chris Hodges, lead pastor, Church of the Highlands, Birmingham, Alabama; author of *Fresh Air* and *Four Cups***

"We live in a generation that craves authenticity. We want real. That's why I'm so excited for Elyse Murphy's book *Confessions of a Church Kid*, which is exactly that—real and authentic. Her honesty is so refreshing, and as someone on my own faith journey, I can definitely relate to the breakthroughs and wisdom she shares. I know this book will bring freedom to all who read it."

—**Francia Raisa, actress, Hollywood, California**

"*Confessions of a Church Kid*, much like my frequent conversations with Elyse, is both playful and profound. Elyse has contended with the unique pressures that come with being raised in a ministry family and has proven that it's possible to see the amusing side of church while remaining honoring, to feel the genuine pain that can occur in relationships while still embracing community, to be brutally authentic while still being graceful . . . in short . . . to be a church kid while still making a remarkable impact in the world. As a church kid myself, and the father of six church kids, I can say with all confidence that this book will be a great benefit to you. I'm so proud of Elyse for sharing her journey with others."

—**Justin Reimer, Oasis Church, Los Angeles, California**

"Our world is obsessed with making sure people know that we 'have it all together.' Unfortunately, this culture has worked its way into the church, and church kids tend to catch the worst of it. This book is a refreshing reminder that none of us really have it all together and it's okay to be honest and transparent. *Confessions of a Church Kid* will bring light into those awkward church-kid places. Elyse lives what she preaches and has a way of communicating that you'll enjoy outrageously. It's about time we heard some confessions from a church kid, and I'm glad Elyse is willing to do so!"

—**Josh, Kelly, youth pastor, Wave Church, Virginia Beach, Virginia**

And if you need more convincing . . .

"*Confessions of a Church Kid* probably ranks among the most riveting, delight-filled, soul-encouraging books ever written. Elyse stands amongst the greats in her literary excellence and style. You'll want to read this book, because I'm her mum and I said so."

—**my Mum, Valery Murphy**

confessions of a Church Kid

HONEST THOUGHTS ON FINDING GOD AND BECOMING MYSELF

ELYSE MURPHY

SALUBRIS℠
RESOURCES

For the one who wants to run,
even when they are injured.

For the one who wants to dance,
even when they have lost their rhythm.

For the one who wants to sing,
even when they have forgotten the lyrics.

This book is for the person wondering if
God can still use them, even though . . .

CONTENTS

FOREWORD 9

INTRODUCTION: CONFESSIONS 11

CONFESSION #1: I HATE CHURCH PEOPLE 15

1   UNINVITED 16

2   NOT FAIR 21

CONFESSION #2: I QUESTION GOD 27

3   O CAPTAIN, MY CAPTAIN 28

CONFESSION #3: I'M NOT QUALIFIED TO BE A CHRISTIAN 35

4   HIKING WITH STRANGERS 36

5   OH, SAY, CAN YOU SEE? 44

CONFESSION #4: I HAVE TO HIDE THE REAL ME 49

6   NEVER BEEN KISSED? *YEAH, RIGHT* 50

7   DRUNK AT A WEDDING 56

CONFESSION #5: I'M CONTROLLED BY FEAR AND ANXIETY 63

8   NIGHT TERRORS 64

9   TERRORIST ATTACKS 70

CONFESSION #6: I'LL BE SINGLE FOREVER 77

10   HEARTBREAK HOTEL 78

11   27 DRESSES 87

CONFESSION #7: I'M NOT PRETTY ENOUGH 95

12   MIRROR, MIRROR 96

CONFESSION #8: I'M LONELY 103

13   MEAN GIRLS 104

CONFESSION #9: I DON'T HAVE A PLAN B 113

14   WHEN I GROW UP 114

CONFESSION #10: IT'S HARD TO TELL THE TRUTH 121

15   LIFE IN THE FAST LANE 122

AFTERWORD: AN HONEST CONFESSION IS A GOOD CONFESSION 129

ACKNOWLEDGEMENTS 135

ABOUT THE AUTHOR 139

FOREWORD

ECENTLY, I HAD THE HONOR of speaking at a conference of thousands of people about some of the more unspoken factors that come along with being a "church kid." You see, like Elyse, I'm a church kid (AKA a normal kid who grew up in church) who has sat in a million different services, sung a million different worship songs, and listened to a million different messages. And while I've *loved* it, I've also got my own story of navigating the challenges, sacrifices, and frustrations.

After I spoke at this conference, the response I received from simply being honest and sharing from my personal experience was way beyond anything I expected. There were so many people who were walking journeys similar to mine, and the truth of my story resonated with them. I couldn't believe how eager they were to share their stories with me. From the young guy who finally felt understood, to the young girl who struggles with having busy pastor parents. From the college girl who thought I was perfect (ridiculous) and couldn't possibly have the sort of anxieties she does, to the young guy who is still trying to figure it all out for himself. From the father in tears who thanked me without any explanation, to the mother who was travailing and anxious about her prodigal child. The stories were endless and almost overwhelming.

Through that experience I realized there's a desperate need for somebody to speak out on behalf of church kids who feel alone, misunderstood, under-valued, and ill-equipped with wisdom for their journey. This is a journey travelled by many, and sadly many are lost along the way. They don't have the support, freedom, and wisdom they need in order to be equipped and empowered to stay the path with Jesus.

I've known Elyse all her life and as long as I can remember, and I'm so proud of the woman of God she is today. I've watched throughout her life as she has made the choices that define her. For this reason, I wholeheartedly believe she's a powerful voice for those who are growing-up in church environments. I believe we church kids are blessed and should never take for granted just how fortunate we are; however, sometimes we just need to know that we aren't in this alone. It's liberating when someone else can give expression to the way we feel.

I hope her words will fall upon your heart, her honesty will be refreshing for your soul, and her wisdom will help you stay on the path that God has uniquely carved out especially for you.

—Laura (Houston) Toggs, Hillsong Church, Sydney, Australia

INTRODUCTION

Confessions

WE LOVE A GOOD CONFESSION. Am I right? We love the quirky, unexpected surprises and unpredictability they bring. We love that everyone has things to confess but pretends they don't. Let's be honest, the very word *confession* makes our ears perk up, our eyes widen, and our bodies lean in a little more. We want the truth . . . with a side of drama. So are you ready for my first confession? Here goes.

Confession: I'm a church kid.

I'm not a huge fan of admitting it, being that "church" people can be a little bit strange, for no good reason. I'd rather be one of the cool kids, you know? Someone who can order an Americano without sugar or cream, who can use the word *literally* in the correct context, and who can be in the same room as Jennifer Lawrence without fangirling. But alas, I was not one of those kids. I literally die when I drink Americanos and cry at the thought of a selfie with J-Law. I'm a church kid. I grew up in church. I practically lived at church. Although my parents were pastors my entire early life, I'm not sure I quite lived up to the expectations of a pastor's kid (PK).

When I was younger I did pretty well. I went to every prayer meeting, every service, and every rehearsal regardless of whether it was relevant to me or not. When I got tired I would just play Snake (the only game on my dad's phone) or fall asleep with one of the other PKs under the front pew. Scandalous, I know.

The older I got, though, the more I realized my role at the church was a big responsibility, and I wasn't sure I was up to the challenge.

Confession: I made for a pretty second-rate church kid.

My brother and sister were much better PKs than I. They both got straight As and had sensible friends. My brother got them by being sweet and smart, and my sister made friends by bossing everybody around (just joking . . . kind of. She's sweet and smart, too. She's just sweet and smart and bossy). Still, somehow, I was always the one causing problems. I had too many questions. I had FOMO (Fear of Missing Out) before it was even a thing. I wanted life to be an adventure. I was curious about who God was and how I could be a Christian and still have fun. And somehow, all of this seemed to be in conflict with the life my parents were creating within the walls of the church. Somehow I always ended up in precarious situations.

Confession: I always worried I would ruin everything
for my parents . . . and maybe for myself.

Cue, dramatic music. I know. I have a flair for the dramatic. I wish my life were a Broadway musical so I could just break into song at any moment. Obviously, everyone around me would join in the chorus with choreography to match. I digress, but actually? I think there's something really healing about confessing the things you feel like you can't admit to anyone. Seriously, you should try it sometime.

You know those things you think in your head but you're afraid to say out loud? Like how you eat Nutella straight from the jar, or how you pretend to understand Indie Culture but you really don't, or how you truly believe you and Katy Perry will be pals someday. Oh wait, just me? Okay.

Either way, I feel better now.

It's like, once the words come out of our mouths, we can take deep breaths. Those admissions don't define us. They don't contain us. They don't trap us. We can move on.

But if you grew up in church, like I did, chances are you don't really feel free to confess how you feel about God, about church, and about life. You probably feel like you have to perform. For some reason, church tends to breed that idea in us. But here's the crazy thing: God doesn't need us to perform. In fact, He doesn't want us to perform. And it isn't until we start to admit the truth about what we think, what we feel, and who we are that we can begin to experience the radical, transforming power of His love.

And it all starts with confession.

Confession: This is harder (and also easier) than it sounds.
Let me guess. Right now you're probably thinking I'm crazy . . . or delusional. Maybe I am (stranger things have happened), but I also have a story about how confession has changed my life. Maybe you'll let me tell it to you. Maybe you'll follow along. Maybe you'll learn alongside me that you don't have to have it all figured out. Maybe, if you get really courageous, you'll read the questions I ask at the end of each section, and attempt to answer them honestly (at least to yourself). Maybe you'll finally allow yourself to say the truth out loud. And maybe . . . just maybe . . . your life will be changed, too.

Confession: I like you already. Let's get started.

Confession #1

I Hate Church People

I HATE CHURCH PEOPLE. Not all of them. I mean, I probably like you. But the "churchy" church people? Blechhhkkk (totally a word). Not a fan. I can't help it. But here's the catch. I love the church. Let me tell you why.

I've grown up in church my whole life, and maybe that's why I can't *stand* church people. You know the kind of people I'm talking about, the ones who have their arms raised perfectly above their heads during worship. Those who are practically schooled in the art of saying "amen" the right number of times during a service—not so many that they seem overboard but not so few they seem too quiet. I never wanted my life to seem that rehearsed. I wanted to be spontaneous and unpredictable.

Maybe that's how I got myself into trouble.

CHAPTER ONE
uninvited

G ROWING UP, I had a birthday each year. In fact, I still do (shocking, I know). In the Murphy household, Mum and Dad would throw each of us kids a birthday party every *second* year. I was always so excited for these parties. I couldn't wait to choose the guest list, the invitations, and the decorations. Mum and I would sit down and create a list of people I wanted to invite, and of course, being a church kid, the nonnegotiable rule was that nobody was to be left out. If I wanted some of the girls in my class to come, I had to invite *all* the girls—even the awkward ones who would buy me the generic brand of Barbie dolls or re-gift a bath spa set. The girls I didn't really want to be at my party. The ones I invited because my mum said so.

Have you ever been to a party and felt like you were *that* kid? The kid who got invited because the birthday girl's parents said so? I have. Except that the party was my church . . . and the birthday kid was a leader.

One night something happened to me. To you it might seem small, but for me? It seemed to define my entire church experience. I'll never forget that night.

I was on my way to a youth group leader's meeting, and as I approached the door I could hear one of the main leaders in my church joking with several students about something. I couldn't hear exactly what he was saying, but I heard him talking about my dad, and the tone in his voice gave me an uneasy feeling in my stomach. This wasn't the first time something like this had happened. "Oh great," I thought to myself, *Here we go again.* I paused, took a deep breath, and rounded the corner.

As soon as I walked in the room, the conversation stopped. The leader looked at me, back at the group, and then back at me. "Uh oh," he finally said, laughing. "We'd better stop talking! The spy just arrived. Anything we say will get back to her dad."

I felt awful and humiliated . . . and about as big an ant. A *baby* ant. This is just one example of dozens of times growing up I felt like I was on one team and the church people were on another. All I wanted was what every kid wants—to fit in. And it seemed to me like a *leader* in our church should be the last person to make me feel like I didn't belong. But there I was—fighting for the attention and approval of this leader.

The more I craved and strived for his acceptance, the less I seemed to have it. I felt jealous when I saw other young people getting the attention I so desperately wanted. I hated the feeling of rejection that overwhelmed me when the "cooler" kids got the opportunities I had asked God for.

I just wanted to feel like I mattered. I wanted to be accepted and noticed. Some nights at church I felt completely ignored.

Throughout high school I had friends in our youth group whom I loved, and I had other youth leaders who loved me and spent time with me, but encouragement from this particular leader was rare and fleeting, which left me feeling like the kid who got an invitation to the party but wasn't really welcome.

As a result, or maybe just as a defense mechanism, I became as critical of church people as I felt they were of me—I hated church people.

Has something like this ever happened to you? Often we become so fixated on the disapproval of one friend, leader, or parent that we become deaf and blind to the encouragement, love, and support that other people offer to us.

Letting Go of the Pain

It took a lot of thinking and praying (and some ugly-crying along the way), but after a while, I finally let God heal my heart. And you know what? I felt freer than I had felt in a long, long time. That moment came at an altar call at a youth retreat. I'll never forget the speaker acknowledging there was "unforgiveness in the room," and I knew he was speaking directly to me. So I made my way down to the front and decided to leave the hurt that had become such a heavy weight on my heart.

I'm not usually a person to get down on my knees, but I knelt down that night and asked God to take away all the pain and confusion and hatred. I felt physically lighter the minute I said the words. For too long I had shut out the pain. In that moment, I learned there's a difference between shutting pain out and letting it go.

When I finally forgave that leader and let go of what he had done, it made me realize that no one is perfect. Not even me . . . *especially* not me! When I admitted that, I felt released from the pressure to be perfect. I suddenly realized that I didn't have to perform for church people, and I didn't need them to perform for me.

> In that moment, I learned there's a difference between shutting pain out and letting it go.

Church people are just people—and we all need Jesus.

Eventually, I reconciled with that leader and saw how God used even the pain I felt in that situation for my good. Seriously, this was like Romans 8:28 playing out in real life for me: "We know that in all things God works for the good of those who love him, who have been called according to his purpose."

Until we let go of past hurts and situations, until we stop feeling responsible for what has happened, until we let go of the insecurity goggles we're wearing (which really don't look cute with *any* outfit), until we let go of the leaders and other church people who have hurt us, we can't let God take control again.

It's possible to trip over something that's behind us.

I can't promise everything will work out for you immediately. For me, it took about five years to see what God was doing. He was taking the pieces of my broken experience and making them new again. You may not see it now, but He wants to do the same for you.

In life things happen that don't make sense. Things confuse us and can even leave us questioning God. The Enemy will use these things to make us bitter, to harden our hearts, and even try to make us decide to give up on the church and church people. Sometimes, the Enemy has succeeded in causing people who are hurt and offended to stop believing in God altogether. Please don't let this happen to you. I really pray you won't.

So . . . what did I learn?

1. I learned that God will build His church—no matter what.

2. I learned that everything we build will be tested. And no matter how pretty, how gold, or how strong it seems on the outside, if it is not centered on God it will implode.

3. No person has the power to break you. This leader didn't break me. Because sin is in the world, there is already brokenness inside each of us. That leader may have brought my insecurities and brokenness to the surface, but God was the One who healed, restored, and brought wholeness.

4. There's a difference between blocking out the pain and letting go of the pain. Holding on to hurt and bitterness only hurts you!

5. I learned that I have some of the biggest cheerleaders that any girl could wish for. And now that my insecurity is out of the way, I can see them!

Open Your Journal

If you've had a situation similar to mine, I pray that you will pull some lessons from your experience like I have from mine. One good way to do this is to journal honestly through your thoughts in a place where no one else will read what you've written. This is the section where I ask you questions and you write the answers in your personal journal. This is your chance to say *exactly* what you want to say, even if you're the only person who ever reads it.

1. While you were reading my story, did a situation from your own life come to mind? Write about it. Try to remember *exactly* who was there, what happened, and how you felt. Hold nothing back.

2. Write a list of people in the church who have offended you and made you angry. Explain why. Be completely honest. (If something has happened to you that was illegal, please tell someone you can trust! Don't keep it to yourself!)

3. For each of the people on your list, imagine what God might be trying to teach you or say to you through that person or that experience.

4. Read Romans 8:28, and write some observations about the verse and how it might apply to your life.

CHAPTER TWO
Not Fair

IT WAS ONE OF THOSE PERFECT, sun-filled, spring afternoons, the ones you want to capture in your mind for the times you're just a little bit stressed and need to get away to your happy place. I was sitting on the balcony of a beautiful hotel room looking over the Port Macquarie waterway at our annual Australian Christian Churches State Conference. I wish you could have seen my view—clear blue water, a beach in the distance, and people the size of ants on their afternoon walks on the track below.

It was the very definition of tranquility, except for the kids playing an extremely loud game of "Marco Polo" in the pool below.

But nothing is perfect.

A New President

Ever since I can remember, my family had been coming to this conference, with us kids starting with the children's programs, graduating to the youth program, and finally having nowhere to go but to the actual conference itself. This particular year I was studying at Hillsong Bible College and had asked for special leave to attend the conference. After all, this was the year my dad was being made president of our church movement for the state of New South Wales (NSW).

My dad had been vice president for ten years, but the past few years he had been managing the movement in the state as the current president was fighting (and winning) his battle against cancer. You could say that Dad had been groomed for this role, and the current president made no secret that he was excited for Dad to take over the role officially.

The day of the official vote arrived, and we were trying not to count our chickens before they hatched, as they say, except we totally had counted them, and we had told everyone how many were hatching—precisely one.

And it was a president chicken.

As we left the hotel room, Dad took one final look over his sermon notes for the new president's address the next evening. I could tell he was nervous. Always the life of the party, he kept a confident face and positive attitude, but he was quieter than usual. He seemed deep in thought.

The business session came—usually known as the session to skip if you wanted to go for a quick surf or coffee—but this year the room stayed full. Everyone wanted to see this historical moment when our new president would be elected.

The executive leadership team was seated at a table on the front stage. Everyone had voted during the break, so all that was left was to count the votes. The moment came, and the sheet of paper with the results was passed to the current president onstage.

That piece of paper looked heavy.

As I sat in the congregation, waiting for the announcement, I felt the weight of this process on my shoulders, the expectation, the last twelve months. I knew it wasn't my name on that piece of paper, but it might as well have been with the way I felt. I felt sick to my stomach and was fighting an urge to run up to the stage and read it for them!

The president looked at the paper and, like any good reality show host, took a dramatic breath in. He then explained the vote was so close that the winner would need to be confirmed by everyone present. Then the announcement: "The winner of the vote and our new state president is (long dramatic pause) . . . Michael Murphy."

Everyone cheered. It was confirmed. The chicken's egg had hatched. He was in. President Dad.

A Terrible Mistake

As one of the leaders gave the financial report, everyone pretended they were listening (while checking their Instagram and returning text messages). Then I noticed something. The piece of paper with the vote tally, the really heavy one, was being passed down the table, and as the leaders looked at it, their faces had three consecutive expressions . . . inquisitive, shock, and horror. The paper was passed down the length of the table.

Finally, the paper was in the hands of the former president. The minute he saw it, he ran offstage (not so inconspicuously, being a large man). An unsettling feeling spread through the crowd. The audience wondered where he had gone. When he returned to the stage, he pulled two people into a "private" conference meeting—my President Dad and the other man who was being considered for the presidency. Now, when I say "private," I mean that it was onstage, in front of a couple thousand people . . . subtle.

Whispers spread through the crowd.

I watched as Dad's expression turned from confidence to confusion to clarity. And then with an empty smile and handshake he returned to the table. My mum stared at my dad with her "What the heck just happened?" face.

The former president took the microphone once again, this time looking like a deer in the headlights, clearly wishing he could run away but knowing there was nowhere to hide. He fumbled, searching for the right words to explain the past few minutes. The tension grew. "I'm so sorry. I read the wrong name. John McMartin actually won the vote; he is the new state president. I'm so sorry."

At first, silence. There was nothing but awkward silence.

As the reality spread throughout the room, people started to ask questions. And then, even worse, people started to ask *me* questions. "Did you hear that?" "Are you okay?" They patted me on the back with impossible amounts of compassion. Their eyes, so many eyes, stared at me. I couldn't look at anyone. I couldn't hear anyone. Dad's gaze searched and found me in the crowd and gave me that empty smile and nod, assuring me everything was going to be okay, even though it felt far from it.

I watched as Dad volunteered to be voted out of the presidency immediately and was the first person to move for the approval of our new state president. Confusing thoughts swirled through my mind. *Had everyone who had claimed to vote for my dad been lying? Was this mistake made on purpose? Could I trust anyone around me?* I wanted to go back in time and fix this. Yes, I wanted to go all Olivia Pope on everybody. I wanted to handle it myself. But I couldn't. The situation was out of my reach. I merely had to endure it. And that sucked . . . big time.

Dad's Amazing Response

I later learned that my dad was as hurt and disappointed as I was, but he was mature enough to realize that although what had happened seemed unfair, it didn't mean everyone was out to get him. In fact, no one was out to get him. Life is full of things that are unfair. The church is full of things that are unfair. But watching my dad respond to this unfair situation with grace taught me how much freedom we find when we stop blaming and mistrusting others just because life isn't fair.

> Life is full of things that are unfair. The church is full of things that are unfair.

That afternoon in the hotel room, it felt like there had been a death in the family. I guess, in a way, there had been. A dream my dad had held for ten years was killed after ten short minutes.

That night my brother and I were on the roster to lead worship. I would rather have adopted a stray cat than lead worship that night, and that's saying something. I hate cats. So Dad sat us down before we left for rehearsal. He had been on the balcony all afternoon, and this was the first I'd heard him talk since the meeting that killed the dream. I honestly thought he was going to tell us to take the night off, that he understood we were upset and the whole thing was completely unfair. Apparently, I didn't know my dad.

Instead, he looked us in the eye and spoke to us, authentically and with complete assurance and authority in his voice. He made sure we knew that while he was disappointed, he was going to be absolutely fine, and, more importantly, so were we. He honored the new president and said that God had called him to do this job and that we were to support him too. He instructed us to go to rehearsal that night ready to worship God. I'll never forget it. He said, "Hold nothing back tonight."

In that moment, I knew we would be okay . . . because Dad had said so.

So . . . what did I learn?

There has probably been a time when something really unfair happened to you or to someone you loved. I'm guessing that, like me, you probably didn't know how to respond. Maybe someone from the church mistreated you, or someone left without warning. Maybe someone exposed a secret you shared with them and you feel like you can never trust anyone again. Let me give you the same advice my dad gave me that night. Hold nothing back from God. People are just people, and life isn't fair, but God loves you and sees your hurt. Here are the things I learned in the midst of my pain.

1. I'm going to be okay. You're going to be okay. How do I know? Because my Dad says so. I'm not talking about my earthly dad, Michael Murphy, right now, though he's pretty much the best ever. I'm talking about the Dad we share . . . our heavenly Father.

2. People are not out to get me. Just because a situation feels unfair doesn't mean anyone was directly at fault. Realizing this has helped me move on and has protected me from feeling bitter toward church people.

3. Expecting others to be perfect only adds to the pressure you feel to be perfect, and no one needs to carry around that type of weight.

4. Move on quickly after a disappointment. Staying down won't help anyone get up, least of all you.

Open Your Journal

If you've had a situation like mine, I pray in the future you might be able to pull some lessons from your experience like I have mine. One good way to do this is to journal honestly through your thoughts in a place where no one else will read what you've written. This is the section where I ask you questions and you write the answers in your personal journal. This is your chance to say *exactly* what you want to say.

1. Describe a time in your life when something happened to you (or someone you love) that felt completely unfair. How did it make you feel? How did you respond? Looking back, was there anyone to blame, or was it just an unfair situation? (Hey, just so you know, sometimes there really is someone to blame. If something wrong or illegal happened to you, please tell someone you trust. Don't keep it hidden.)

2. Do you feel like you have unrealistic expectations of yourself or others?

3. Go back through those expectations and see how you can change those expectations to be more realistic.

Confession #2

I Question God

WHEN PEOPLE ASK ME what superpower I wish I had (wait—people don't ask you that on the regular?), I always tell them the same thing. It's not flying. It's not being invisible. It's not even shooting spiderwebs out of my wrists, although . . .

If I could have any superpower, it would be perspective.

I would love the ability to leave my current situation and see it in the grand scheme of my life. You just changed your superpower to mine didn't you? It's okay. I'll share.

Often life doesn't make any sense. When I'm right in the middle of a difficult situation, I'm sure God has gotten it wrong. Many times I think I've heard from Him about something He wants me to do or something that is supposed to happen. But when those things don't work out the way I thought they would, it makes me wonder: *Is He still there? Did He forget about me? Did I ever hear Him in the first place?*

How much less time would we spend being anxious, stressed, upset, and confused if we could just see how everything works out in the end? I'd be willing to bet that we would gain at least a few years of our lives.

But maybe, just maybe, instead of wishing for superpowers, we could learn to trust God even when life doesn't make sense. Easier said than done though, right?

CHAPTER THREE

O Captain, My Captain

EVER FELT LIKE you were born for something, over-quoting the "for such a time as this" Bible verse with the best of them and certain you were going to accomplish *that thing*, only to miss out? Yep. Me, too.

Years ago I watched Paul Hanna, an older student at my school, deliver one of the most moving speeches I've ever witnessed. I didn't know Paul at the time, but he was my school captain (student body president), and this was his final speech of the year. No pressure, right?

As he neared the end of his speech, he stopped. Tears were in his eyes. We all waited in anticipation. Searching for the words before he proclaimed them, he said, "I'm not speaking to you as your captain right now but as a fellow student. I want to talk to you about Jesus." The whole room was silent. There he stood, vulnerable before the school. He was leaving a legacy and was inspiring me to leave mine.

So the dream was birthed in me as a little girl in grade four. I was going to leave my mark. I was going to be captain.

Fast-forward seven years.

I had been on every school council committee possible, had represented the school well at extra curricular activities, and was in good standing with most people in my grade. I was getting good grades, was publicly known as a Christian, and made it no secret that I wanted to be captain. I was on track to secure the position.

A few weeks before the captaincy votes started, the predictions began. The odds were on me to get captain and one of my best friends, Kelly, to get vice-captain. This was going to be the perfect combination. Kelly and I used to dream and plot together at summer camp every year how we were going to force people in our school to become Christians.

Key word: *force*. Whether they liked it or not, they were meeting Jesus. How endearing of us, I know.

There were five rounds to the voting process, and with each round, the tension and pressure would build as the number of applicants diminished. The first round was the nominations. As prearranged, Kelly nominated me and I nominated her. Genius, I know! The second round was the vote. Our whole grade voted on prefects, the team of people who would assist the captain. Once you were voted to be a prefect, you were eligible to become captain. This is the only reason I ever wanted to be a prefect, and I'm pretty sure the only reason *anyone* wants to be prefect. I mean who wants to be on the team when they can be the leader? Oh right, the whole humility thing. Guess I missed that. Anyway, I just prayed I wouldn't get stuck as prefect.

To our delight, we both made it through to prefects. Like reaching the "safe level" on *Who Wants to Be a Millionaire*. My candidacy had been confirmed. All I needed was my bow and arrows, and I was going to go Katniss Everdeen on this thing. Again, I probably missed a few things in my passion to be captain, like not trying to kill people off.

In the third round of the competition, the nominees gave speeches. It was a would-be reality show with a million opportunities to make a fool of yourself and get voted off the island or killed (too far?). But I wasn't worried. I had the talent (I was good at giving speeches) and the motives (I wanted to leave a Paul Hanna legacy), and it seemed to me that God wanted this for me as well. Surely this was His will. Nothing was going to stop me from achieving it.

I spent hours in my room preparing, practicing, and asking Dad to help me write my speech. I was ready to leave my legacy! Of course this wasn't the time to be giving my Jesus speech like Paul Hanna did. This was a time to speak to a better tomorrow, a brighter future, and Red Bull in the drinking fountains.

Yes. We. Can!

The Waiting Game

For the fourth round of the competition, we had to represent our school at an event. This was a chance to be a "trial" captain. While the responsibilities varied, depending on the event, mostly it was about smiling, shaking hands, and making the school look good. The most coveted event to cover was the graduation ball, a big dressy event celebrating the previous year's graduating seniors. Everyone wanted to go to this event because the prefects got to sit at a table with the

principal and discuss the plans for the next year. I wanted to go because
I would get to wear a pretty dress (and the senior guys were super
cute), but I wouldn't let that overshadow my opportunity to impress
the principle with the "make good choices" advice I was determined
to give (loudly) to all seniors in earshot. Add to *all* of that, it seemed
that the prefects who went to the graduation ball were always a shoo-
in for captain, and I love shoes.

Unfortunately, I wasn't sent to that event. Devastating, I know.
Instead, I was invited to the women's liberation event, where I sat
around listening to a bunch of boring speakers ramble on about things
that would have seemed important to me if I hadn't been so caught
up on getting elected captain. I wanted to be at the graduation ball! I
should have been at that graduation ball!

I wanted to show how poised and gracious and mature I could be.
I wanted everyone to know I had what it took to be captain.

Although I wasn't invited to attend the graduation ball, the unofficial
consensus from our grade still placed the odds in my favor. Kelly and
I kept dreaming about all the things we could accomplish and how
much fun we would have. Teachers even stopped us in the hallway
to give us a wink here and a nudge there or an outright "is it too early
to congratulate you for captain yet?"

Yes, it was. But I didn't care.

The fifth round was the panel interview. The tension was growing,
and so was the competitive nature of those trying to become captain.
The day of the interviews, we were all sitting in drama class, rehearsing
a play. Surprisingly, or perhaps not so surprisingly, all the female
prefects trying for captain were in drama together.

One by one we were called to the principal's office. One by one
we returned, facing an interrogation. If a girl came back reporting
the interview had gone well, we pretended to be overjoyed for her.
If she came back upset, we feigned sympathetic looks. Finally, my
name was called. I don't remember a lot of the interview, but I do
remember there seemed to be more panel members than the other
girls had mentioned. Was that a good thing? Were they doing a final
check with the decision committee before they offered me the position
of captain then and there?

I left the office and remember saying a quick prayer as I walked
back to the drama room to face the cross-examination.

"Jesus, I've done my bit. Now Your will be done."

After that day we waited . . . and waited . . . and waited. After two weeks of no news and checking daily at the front office, we began to get restless. Then, in the final class of the day (drama, drama, drama!) a note arrived.

"The principal will phone each of the captain applicants this afternoon."

We looked at each other. No one spoke. That afternoon I would know. Would I have the chance to be the school captain like Paul Hanna or just another prefect no one remembered? I was so nervous I couldn't concentrate or sit still.

The bell rang, and we needed no encouragement to pack up quickly. After ceremoniously saying our "good-lucks," we went our separate ways, knowing full well that tomorrow the process would finally be over.

All going to plan, I would be captain.

And the winner is . . .

Ring, Ring. Ring, Ring.

This was it. The moment I had dreamed about since I was ten years old.

"Hello?" I tried to sound confident and composed but knew I was neither. And my shaky voice gave me away.

"Hello Elyse, it's Mr. Burgess here."

After some pointless small talk and niceties, there was a pause. Not a short, shallow pause but a long, drawn-out, heart-attack kind of pause.

"Elyse, I'm going to ask you to stay prefect next year. We have chosen another girl for captain."

"Okay. See you tomorrow, sir."

Dreams . . . shattered.

I put down the phone and physically felt my gut drop as I crumpled in a mess on the kitchen floor. I had wanted this and carried the weight of it more than I was even aware. I stayed there trying to gain control, finally releasing my knees from my chest once I was too tired to cry anymore. This may sound like an overreaction, but at the time all I could think about was how I thought being captain was what God wanted me to do. *Had I heard Him wrong? Had I heard Him right, and He had failed me? Had I failed Him? Why did He let me want it so much if it was never going to happen?* I was confused, gutted, and lost.

Lying on my bed, I found myself going over and over the whole process, wondering what more I could have done. And then I remembered the prayer. The small, seemingly insignificant prayer I had prayed as I came out of my interview: "Jesus, I've done my bit. Now Your will be done."

> In that moment I realized that although I had many questions, I didn't have to hide them. God welcomed my questions.

Lying there on my tear-soaked bed, it hit me . . . maybe "God's plan" for next year was completely different than the plan I had created for myself. Maybe it wasn't that I hadn't heard God correctly but that I hadn't heard everything yet. Maybe the things I had heard, I had misapplied. Either way, in that moment I realized that although I had many questions, I didn't have to hide them. God welcomed my questions. He just wanted me to trust that the answers would come in good time if I kept walking with Him . . . even when it didn't make sense to me.

Over the next twelve months, the answers *did* come.

While being captain seemed like everything to me during the election process, there was no way I could foresee what the next twelve months would hold for me. A year of spontaneous after-school adventures with my friends. A year of focused attention on my final exams. A year of happiness and a year of heartbreak, of late-night phone calls and my own brush with fame. When I look back, I don't think I could have given the captain position the time and energy that our captain gave it, and she did a great job.

If I had the choice to go back again, I wouldn't change a thing. Actually, maybe I would chill out on the whole Katniss, Hunger Games thing. I might change that. But nobody's perfect.

I learned that God's "no" is actually a hidden passage to the door of His "I have something better."

He is faithful.

So . . . what did I learn?

Hey, you know that opportunity you missed out on, that person you didn't get to meet, that spot on the team you didn't qualify for, that friend who unexplainably stopped talking to you? None of it is outside God's plan for you. You may not understand it right now—I know I didn't—but maybe it's God's way of saying, "Hang in there. I can see you. I see you from where I am, and I have something better for you."

Here are a few things I learned from my own experience with disappointment.

1. We can't always foresee the future, and even if we could, we wouldn't necessarily make the right choices. Even if I had seen what was coming in the future, I might still have chosen to be captain, to my detriment. God sees the future and He protects us, and I'm grateful for that.

2. God's timing is perfect. That isn't just a cliché. We need to be okay with not knowing everything all the time.

3. God has promised me a life beyond my wildest dreams. I need to learn to trust where He is leading me.

4. God is not surprised by my disappointments. He can handle my hurts and my questions. I just need to learn to listen for His answers.

5. If I let a confusing situation stop me from hearing God's voice, I miss out on the "something better" He has for me.

Open Your Journal

If you've had a situation like mine, I pray in the future you might be able to pull some lessons from your experience like I have from mine. One good way to do this is to journal honestly through your thoughts in a place where no one else will read what you've written. This is the section where I ask you questions and you write the answers in your personal journal. This is your chance to say *exactly* what you want to say.

1. Have you ever felt like God promised something that you didn't get? Write about the situation and about how it made you feel.

2. Is it possible that, in hindsight, God has something better for you? Allow yourself to write and dream about the possibilities.

3. Write a list of three things you're grateful for (My name is spelled E-L-Y . . . oh, just kidding).

4. Look up Romans 5:4–5 (preferably in *The Message*). What is God saying to you today from this passage of Scripture?

Confession #3

I'm Not Qualified to Be a Christian

SOMETIMES I FEEL LIKE the world's biggest mess-up. To start, 87 percent of the time I'm saying something or doing something that makes me feel like a complete idiot. The other day I thought I was eating a mint only to find out it was a Tylenol. It did *not* freshen my breath. #accidentaldruguse. I might just be the reason there are blonde jokes in the world.

As if that weren't bad enough, I constantly make the kinds of mistakes that give Christians a bad name. You know that verse in Romans 7 where Paul talks about how he wants to do the things he can't do and how he always finds himself doing the things he doesn't want to do?

Yeah. That's me. Maybe it's you, too.

CHAPTER FOUR

Hiking with strangers

H ERE'S THE DEAL. I like being a girl. I have ever since I can remember. The fact that we can cry whenever we want without needing a reason, that we have the ability to sweet-talk our way out of a parking ticket (don't pretend like you haven't tried it), and the universal understanding that we take a long time to get ready—it's all just so convenient.

In my opinion, being a girl is so much fun (minus the whole giving birth issue, but I'll cross that bridge when I come to it).

So, as you can imagine, being a self-admitted "girly girl," I'm not really one to jump at an opportunity to go hiking with a bunch of strangers. And yet that's the exact position I found myself in a few years ago.

Dad had to select a couple of young people from our church to represent our local area as a part of a documentary to be aired on a national news program. The purpose of the documentary was to give the next generation an opportunity to recognize and pay tribute to the Australians who fought in World War II. This group of young people would travel to Malaysia with three politicians to walk the Sandakan Death March. (I know, encouraging name, right?)

To give you some context for the hike, during World War II, over 2,000 Australian soldiers who were prisoners of war were forced to walk to their death through the Sandakan trail in Borneo. The soldiers walked more than 162 miles, and this team would walk 62 miles of that trail. Each person would carry a photo and a short biography of one of the prisoners of war. At the point on the trail where the hiker's assigned soldier had died, the hiker would get up and tell the soldier's story.

Reliving the stories of these soldiers and paying respect to the fallen men would be absolutely incredible. But the physical activity? Not so much.

When Dad asked my advice about whom he should send, I wasted no time in listing 534 names of people who would be perfect for that kind of thing, deliberately trying to steer his thoughts away from myself. There was *no* way I was going! But it was too late; his mind had already gone there, and although I tried everything I could to talk him out of it, he decided it would be a brilliant idea to send me.

Me: the girl whose idea of camping under the stars was staying in a five-star hotel, the girl whose idea of roughing it was to stay in the same outfit the entire day. This had to be some kind of cruel joke. What had I ever done wrong to deserve this punishment? He was sending me to my death. The Sandakan Death March—what kind of parent would do such a thing?

To Make Matters Worse

At our first team meeting, local politician Scott Morrison explained that there were a couple of items of clothing we would need to get in order to "survive" this trip. *Survive?* I thought to myself. *Well, I guess I've had a good twenty-one years of life so far.*

We would need hiking boots, hiking shorts, and, worst of all, Crocs. *Crocs!* C-R-O-C-S! I wanted to run out of the room screaming at the top of my lungs. You see, I was the person who judged people for wearing Crocs! (Just quickly, for those who think I'm talking about wearing a baby crocodile on my foot, chill out. Crocs have been advertised as the ugliest, yet most comfortable, shoe ever created.)

To be honest, I wondered why a good, honest, socially contributing citizen would ever think it appropriate to wear Crocs on her feet in public. And now, as the Lord would have it, I was being told I needed not only to purchase a pair but also to endure a week of wearing them—in public . . . with *socks!* I was convinced I was being pranked—either that or I had landed in a horror version of *The Truman Show* and I was Jim Carrey.

I was devastated. I would get hiking boots if they forced me to. I would even borrow hiking shorts and pack them (so Mum would be happy). But there was *no way* I was getting a pair of Crocs. Well, apparently this *was* a horror film, and I *was* getting Crocs. I figured it was the latest type of torture. Fine, if I was absolutely forced into the worst possible situation of wearing Crocs *and* socks, I would wear them *a-la-Elyse:* They would be pink, and I would accompany them with frilly, lacy, white socks. Take that, Truman people!

After two weeks of bargaining, pleading, and shamelessly manipulating to get out of going on this trip, the night before our departure arrived. My bag was packed with a hair straightener (just in case), Barbie Band-Aids, and brand-new make-up so I would still look like a rock star even if I fell down a cliff. As I sat on my bag and forced it closed, I began to realize what I was in for: hiking sixty-two miles through the Malaysian jungle with a group of people I didn't know, none of whom had blonde hair or were as concerned as I was about the lack of personal hygiene.

> There I was, a twenty-one-year-old pastor who preached about overcoming obstacles, crying and begging my mum not to make me go.

To make matters *even* worse, every embarrassing moment would be captured forever on film.

I started to cry. Not a one-glistening-tear-rolling-down-my-cheek cry but a full-throttle-puffy-red-eyes-can't-catch-my-breath cry.

There I was, a twenty-one-year-old pastor who preached about overcoming obstacles, crying and begging my mum not to make me go.

The truth? I was scared. As I sat there on the floor that night, emotionally exhausted, I felt completely unqualified. Have you ever felt like that? Like you were stuck in a situation that, no matter how hard you tried, there was no way out of. Where you felt like no matter how hard you tried, you weren't going to be successful.

Once I caught my breath, I prayed a long, powerful, spiritual prayer that went something like this: "God, You got me into this. So it's your fault if I die. Deal?"

And I went to sleep. By *sleep*, I mean I lay awake in my bed thinking about all the possible ways a snake could eat me. Obviously.

I didn't think the situation could possibly get any worse, but when I arrived at the airport the next morning, I realized I was mistaken. First, it was 4:00 a.m., and no one in their right mind is awake at that hour. On top of that, as I approached the "team," I realized how different every single person was.

The first kid I noticed was jumping up and down, holding and drinking simultaneously from *two* extra-large energy drinks—one in each hand. I'm sure that with more hands, he would have had more energy drinks. I fought every urge not to slap him, then and there. I looked around for any other girls who looked remotely similar to me. There were three girls, but they weren't like me at all. They were about five years younger than me, in their own little clique, listening to their iPods and talking about Marilyn Manson. (I would much rather have talked about Marilyn Monroe.)

Finally, my friend Jimmy arrived. Jimmy and I grew up together in church, and I figured he was the closest thing to Tarzan, so he could protect me from the aforementioned snake attacks/death. Also, he hated Crocs too, so we understood each other. I ran up to him, and we laughed as we wondered what we had gotten ourselves into. But inside, I wasn't laughing. Every single person was different—everyone was a different age, and represented a different background, upbringing, or religion.

There was no common ground.

A Surprising Discovery

The plane trip was the very picture of peace and unity (insert copious amounts of sarcasm here). Liam (energy-drink boy) wriggled around incessantly in his seat from an excess of caffeine in his system (shocker), kicking the back of mine. I sat on my hands to stop myself from strangling him and tried to enjoy watching *The Notebook* one more time before all modern technology and Ryan Gosling were ripped away from me for two full weeks and I was forced to actually converse with these people.

After a brief moment of crisis—the kind of crisis that involved leaving my passport on the airplane, freaking out, going back the next day, and retrieving my passport (thanks, Jesus)—the hike began.

Initially, the whole thing was one big blur of walking, crossing rivers, climbing mountains, sweating, fighting more urges to hurt Liam, and not showering. But then I started to get the hang of it. Up the hill . . . down the hill (fetch the pail of water?). As the first day came to a close, we ascended our final hill. On the other side, I looked up for a moment and found myself in awe of a spectacular view.

Sadly, in my moment of wonder, I forgot to look where I was going. The next thing I knew, I had lost my footing and was plummeting to my death. Well, not really my "death," but it was a hard fall and not something a Barbie Band-Aid could fix.

I landed on my wrist with a bruised face and eyes full of tears.

The guide carried me down the mountain and, of course, the

cameras caught the drama of the day in perfect view. As I sat at the doctor's office that night, waiting for the X-ray and nearly fainting at the slight touch of my hand, I felt like giving up more than ever. The doctor came out and confirmed that I had sprained my wrist and explained that while it was possible to carry on, he wouldn't recommend it. Believe it or not, that was *exactly* what I needed to hear.

Something rose up inside of me when I heard the doctor say I shouldn't continue. Suddenly I *knew* I could do it. Granted, a large portion of my determination probably came from my don't-tell-me-what-to-do stubbornness kicking in. Whatever it was, giving up seemed too easy. I had an injury, yes, but I had a determination to keep going. There was no way anyone was going to tell me to stop this hike.

I had flown all this way, and I was not about to go home now! Plus, I'd eaten too many carbs the final week of preparation that I still needed to work off. (The mind of a female is a mysterious thing.)

I wrapped up my arm, took some painkillers and went to sleep, more determined than ever to prove the doctor wrong.

I'm not going to lie. The next few days were tough. There was pain and more falls on my already damaged wrist. But pushing through all that, I began to realize something: *I was actually starting to have some fun.* Only little bits at first, but as I let go of my judgments, my prejudices, and my need to shower, I also began to feel positive about the stories we were all writing together. I began to feel genuine respect, empathy, and emotion for the World War II soldiers who had endured such terrible hardship so that I could live in freedom.

> We were all unqualified, but we were all in this together.

With each soldier's story, I learned other stories too. I learned the stories of the people walking this journey with me, and as I learned their stories, I realized I wasn't the only one who was unqualified. We were *all* unqualified, but we were all in this together.

I learned the story of a young boy who had just moved to Australia as a refugee and hardly spoke English but wanted a better life for his family. I learned the story of a young girl who was misunderstood at school and seen as a rebellious troublemaker, when all she wanted was a bit of attention. At home she got the opposite. I learned the story of a Muslim boy who felt like he could never talk to Christians because of the judgment heaped on him. The day I listened to his story and he listened to mine, we felt a release of prejudice from both of us, and we became friends.

We were all just people with stories, and as we learned each other's stories, our friendship grew. Eventually we became a family—a weird, slightly strange, and kind of offensive family, but I think that's the best kind.

I'll never forget crossing that finish line. These people who started as aliens to me had become my *family*. We slowed down until we were together, and we crossed that finish line as one. We had done it together . . . Crocs and all.

So . . . what did I learn?

That trip changed my life, and I learned more things than I have time to write. If I had to condense them to a short list, here are a few things I learned:

1. I'm not the only one who feels unqualified. We all feel unqualified at some point to meet the task at hand (whether it's a hike, an exam, or a relationship). Here's the deal: I'm not qualified to be a Christian. But no one is. That's why we need Jesus.

2. We need each other. On this trip I learned the value of doing things together. In Australia we call this "mateship," the bond that forms between two people that makes them less like friends and more like family. If I had tried to complete the journey by myself, I'm pretty sure I would still be stumbling through the Malaysian jungles by myself . . . with my Crocs . . . and my frilly socks.

3. We will get tired and even hurt, but sometimes the bravest and best thing we can do is to keep walking.

4. We have a responsibility to look out for others, to recognize when someone else is struggling and come alongside to help them out. After all, it won't be long before we'll need someone to do the same for us. That's how I survived this sixty-two-mile hike through the jungle. It's how I thrive in my walk with Jesus. And it's how we can bring positive changes to this generation and to our world. Together, we can do it. Because together we're better.

Open Your Journal

If you've had a situation like mine, I pray in the future you might be able to pull some lessons from your experience like I have from mine. One good way to do this is to journal honestly through your thoughts in a place where no one else will read what you've written. This is the section where I ask you questions and you write the answers in your personal journal. This is your chance to say *exactly* what you want to say.

1. We all have times when we feel like we don't have what it takes. Are you going through something right now that makes you feel unqualified? Do you feel like there is no way out? Write about it in your journal.

2. Does anybody know what you're walking through? If not, whom could you tell? Write down two or three people, the type of people who will cheer you on even when you're tired and sore. And hey, don't say there's no one! And now? Call one or all of those people. Just do it.

3. Make a list of the things you need in order to feel "qualified" for your current circumstances (like courage, intelligence, or a certain skill set), and then tell God you want those things. Make a list of practical things you could do to improve your skills in that area.

4. Read Matthew 7:7 and write down what you think the Holy Spirit is saying to you.

CHAPTER FIVE

Oh, Say, Can You See?

HOPPED OFF THE PLANE AT LAX *with my dreams and a cardigan...*"
Truer words could not have been sung over the loudspeaker of
the plane as we touched down in Los Angeles. I was living that
song. Except for the cardigan. Instead, I had my brother's hand-me-
down waterproof overcoat and about ten layers of clothing underneath
... just in case they lost my luggage or I accidentally got on a flight to
Antarctica. Thanks, Mum! This was my first time traveling by myself,
and I was going to be gone for a whole month. For a sheltered church
kid, the excitement was almost unbearable. My final destination was
on the East Coast of America, in Virginia Beach. I was flying to hang out
with my best friend and her family. (This must have been my parents'
way of giving me independence while making sure I didn't get arrested,
touché.) But before my next flight, I had a few hours to kill in LA ... a
few hours *alone* in an unknown city.

Or, as I saw it, *freedom!*

Now that I had flown from Australia to America, my first job as
an independent traveler was to get through the ever-unpredictable
ordeal of customs. I felt like a little girl playing grown-up. In the line,
I began to practice how I should act, trying to find a suitable mix of
"confident" and "independent" while maintaining that certain sense
of adorable innocence. I rehearsed my best "not guilty" face, which
was a cross between smiling for an awkward high school photo and
badly needing to go to the bathroom.

Nevertheless, I made it through customs. Success!

I ungracefully heaved my suitcases onto a luggage cart and
maneuvered it to the exit (maneuvered is a generous word, since of
course my cart had one wobbly wheel, which made steering nearly
impossible). The airport doors flung open. I felt the sting of rain on my

face, blurring my vision while my hair blew as if creating its own mini tornado. I couldn't see a thing. But I didn't care. After fifteen hours on a plane, it felt heavenly.

I got my bearings and discovered I needed to walk about ten minutes to get to my terminal. I had the option of taking a shuttle bus, but being confined to another enclosed space for *any* amount of time after that fifteen- hour flight really wasn't an option . . . unless Zac Efron was on the bus, which of course he wasn't. So I decided to walk.

Be Aggressive . . . Be Aggressive!

As I started my trek to the terminal, I was completely overwhelmed by this new, chaotic environment. There was a sea of yellow "cabs" (we call them "taxis") on the road. People were screaming at each other to hurry up and screaming at *me* to watch where I was going, and I felt like I needed to scream at someone just to fit in. It quickly became clear that no one here cared about my personal walking space. If I was going to reach my terminal before lunchtime tomorrow, I was going to have to be a little more aggressive. So I was, gladly.

And it worked! Here's a hint for your next LA trip. Apparently, if you don't smile and you walk at a fast pace, people think you know where you're going.

After about fifteen minutes of near misses and dirty looks from oncoming pedestrians, I reached my terminal.

My next task? Get myself and my luggage to the departures check-in desk . . . *located on level two.*

More Difficult Than You Think

I decided to take the escalator. This was mistake number one.

I pushed my luggage cart (my luggage weighed more than I did) onto the escalator and, like a weight lifter at the Olympics, put myself into a squat/lunge position, raising my arms above my head to hold it in place. This was mistake number two.

It didn't take long for me to realize that I was not an Olympic weight lifter. It also didn't take me long to realize this was going to be a short-lived trip because I was about to experience death by luggage-crushing. I held the luggage in place as long as I could, shaking at the knees and elbows. The weight was forcing my body position lower and lower, until one knee was shaking but still upright, which is more than I can say for the other knee.

My other knee was in some kind of newly invented yoga position, stretching past my back, seemingly trying to make its way back down the escalator. My eyes were shut tight. I couldn't watch what I had already decided would be my final moments of life.

Although I felt the end of the escalator drawing near, there was no time to warn my body, so I just decided to hang on for dear life. I opened my eyes in time to see the cart tip over the end of the escalator and dive onto the cement ground, followed quickly by my bags, which immediately sprang open for all the world to see.

I dove onto the casualties of my suitcases, scooping up my belongings as if my life depended on it. And of course, as far as I was concerned, my life *did* depend on it (my entire underwear collection had decided to kamikaze out onto the floor). I shot a look around to make sure no one was walking by to see my mess of a situation, but as I did, I caught a glimpse of myself in the mirror wall. What an image!

What had happened to me? I was a sweaty, disheveled mess with a red, runny nose and hair that looked like a bird's nest. This is not what I imagined I would look like on my glamourous trip to LA. As I sat looking at myself in the mirror, attempting to fix the hot mess of a hairstyle before me, something moved.

There was movement in the mirror, and it wasn't my reflection.

I sat up and squinted, peering into the mirror as intently as I could. That's when I saw it. This mirror wasn't a mirror . . . it was a tinted window! I had just been Australian entertainment for about 100 Americans whose flight had been delayed!

At least they found it funny.

Welcome to America!

So . . . what did I learn?

Surely there was no lesson to be learned from this disaster, right? Wrong. I learned several important lessons that day.

1. Don't take yourself too seriously. There was a time in my life when something like this would have devastated me, and I would have taken months to recover. It's true I didn't bounce back right away after this embarrassment; it took a long hot shower and a nice cup of coffee for that to happen. Before long I was sharing my story as a fun response when people asked how my trip was.

2. Take the bus. Even if Zac Efron isn't on it.

3. I need to learn to laugh at myself. There are times when I least expect it—and usually when I'm being a little too arrogant for my own good—that life reminds me that I'm not as smooth as I think I am. And maybe . . . that's true for you, too.

Open Your Journal

If you've had a situation like mine, I pray in the future you might be able to pull some lessons from your experience like I have from mine. One good way to do this is to journal honestly through your thoughts in a place where no one else will read what you've written. This is the section where I ask you questions and you write the answers in your personal journal. This is your chance to say *exactly* what you want to say.

1. Recall a time that was really embarrassing for you. Write the whole story, and try to spin it in a way that's funny. If you look at it with the right perspective, you'll be able to have a good laugh.

2. Read Micah 6:8 (in *The Message* if possible) and you'll see that not taking yourself too seriously is biblical.

3. Make a list of things that make you feel unqualified. As you reflect on your list, laugh at the goodness of God that He uses you despite these quirks and shortcomings!

4. Get a cup of coffee with a friend and laugh. Sometimes the best way to put life back into perspective is to enjoy a good laugh.

> Sometimes the best way to put life back into perspective is to enjoy a good laugh.

Confession #4

I Have to Hide the Real Me

I HAD A MASQUERADE PARTY for my twenty-first birthday. Of course, since I was the birthday girl, I had the best mask. My mask was painted on (think: Drew Barrymore in *Ever After*). As I walked around the party, every now and then I stopped and asked people to take off their masks because I couldn't tell who they were—even some of my best friends!

This makes for a fun party . . . but not such a fun life.

So often I'm walking around life as if I'm still at that birthday party. I'm scared to take off my mask, in case people don't like what they see. There are a million reasons I do this: insecurity . . . fear . . . and usually, shame. But wearing a mask only makes us feel more afraid, more ashamed, and more insecure. What we often forget is that our prettiest mask may fool everyone around us, but we can never fool God.

Here's the good news. The *real* you, the one you're hiding, is the one He loves best.

CHAPTER SIX

Never Been Kissed? Yeah, Right.

KNOW COUPLES WHO DIDN'T KISS until their wedding day. If I were wearing a hat, I would take it off to them. I truly admire people who have this strong conviction and exercise the willpower to stick with it. Unfortunately, hats don't look so good on me, and I also don't have that kind of willpower (or maybe I do and I just haven't exercised it).

Now, don't get me wrong. I don't go around kissing people I don't know (at least not too often), but I can't say I have never been kissed. Sorry, Dad!

Thank goodness, I also don't know anyone who doesn't laugh or go tomato-red when they share the story of their first kiss. Let's be honest. It's awkward, uncomfortable, and just plain weird. Who decided that putting our faces together and tilting our heads slightly in opposite directions would be considered a romantic gesture? Add that to the awkwardness of trying this strange movement for the first time, and you get enough laughable stories to last a lifetime.

I remember the first time I was kissed . . . *actually* kissed. Not the time when I was fifteen years old and my crush at school brushed (possibly smacked) my mouth with his mouth; you could hardly call *that* a kiss. It lasted 0.000005 of a second and was rudely interrupted by my friend's dad announcing that the "party pies" were ready and the games were about to begin (romantic, right?).

This was not that time. This was the *real* time. And although I wish it were as endearing as Drew Barrymore's experience in *Never Been Kissed*—I can't say it was even a fraction that adorable.

High School Crush

There was a boy in the grade below me (I know, I'm a cradle robber) whom I'd had a crush on for a while. He was in a band. Enough said.

We would talk at school between classes, and after school we would "chat" on MSN using a myriad of emoticons and corny quotes. This is how dating was done when I was in high school, before every high school student had his or her own phone to text.

I had been told he might like me, and I'm pretty sure I did a terrible job of hiding the fact that I liked him, too. Anyone walking by could see I'd already picked out the church where we would get married. After weeks of distant flirtation, which was exciting and actually quite comfortable for me, our school was hosting a music performance night, and we were both going to be there. This meant we would have to hang out in close proximity. Yikes!

He, of course, was playing keyboard (so hot), and we would shamelessly flirt between performances. By "flirt" I mean I would awkwardly laugh at anything he said, whether he was joking or not, and sway like I was about to pee my pants. I realized as we were spending time together in person that I was way better when I could think about my response before typing it into the computer. Now, however, I was feeling uncomfortable with conversing in real time. Think of a teenage version of Tina Fey, add a couple of pounds for awkwardness, and you're not too far off.

Of course, I couldn't *tell* him (or anyone else) I was uncomfortable, so I had to play it off like I had done this a thousand times before.

Still, for some reason it was working. We found ourselves together for most of the night, whispering and laughing. At one stage he even grazed my hand with his. Scandalous church kid.

Then he did something that made my stomach jump into my throat. He told me to meet him after the music night on the ramp just below the auditorium. And *everyone* knew what happened on the ramp just below the auditorium.

In one sense, I *wanted* to meet him because I felt like that would make me a grown-up. I knew it would earn me the respect of my friends and also make me feel like I was attractive and likable (plus, he was cute and played the keyboard). But if I was being honest, kissing a boy wasn't something the real Elyse Murphy did. And part of me knew that meeting him there would be crossing a personal line for me. I wasn't ready.

To Kiss or Not to Kiss

I waited until he left the room before I slowly walked to the ramp. I still wasn't sure I wanted to go, but I also didn't want to be "that girl" who turned away the invite of a cute boy. If I knew one thing (and truly, I only knew one thing) it was that these opportunities don't come along every day. Who knew how long it would be before I had my next opportunity?

As I turned the corner, my heart was beating faster than it had ever beaten before, but I reasoned with myself. *This is not that big of a deal* (even though I knew it was). *It's just a kiss. (Is there really such thing as "just" a kiss?) He's a cute boy. (But does he even care about me?) I'm going to get my first kiss. (Do I truly want it?)*

To make things more confusing, I knew my mum was already on her way to pick me up, so I only had a little bit of time.

When I saw him, my decision was made. After all, his hat was on sideways, and in the last few minutes he had found a skateboard and was standing on it, talking to another girl. As soon as I walked up, she walked away, as if she knew what was about to happen. I tried to lower my voice and sound really calm, saying, "Hey there." Instead, I caught my shoe on a rock and half-tripped down the ramp to where my sweaty palms landed in his, and he kept me from falling.

We stood there laughing and mumbling words neither of us could understand for what seemed like forever. *How romantic.*

I knew my mum would be calling me soon to tell me she was out front. Plus, families were starting to leave the auditorium. We didn't have much time. I had no idea how this whole thing was meant to work, but knew I needed to pretend I was an expert. I just kept laughing and mumbling and looking down at his feet. *Did I think I was meant to kiss his feet?* Who knows?

Finally, after what seemed like ages, he lifted up my head. With my final bit of resolve, I resisted against his hand. He kept lifting harder and harder and, finally, I gave in. I stared into his eyes.

I was terrified. These were unchartered waters . . . illegal waters.

He leaned forward until he almost fell off his skateboard. Since I didn't know I was supposed to close my eyes I just stared at his eyelids and wondered if I was going to hell for this. Oh well. Too late now!

I would describe the rest, but I think I've painted a pretty good picture so far, and I don't want to get too graphic. It was awful. What made it even more traumatic was that since we were right under the streetlight, we were in perfect view of *all my mom's friends.* Subtle.

Suddenly my phone started vibrating and I knew Mum was here.

What happened next sounded like a good idea in my head, but all it did was prove that I watch way too many Disney movies. I fled the scene. In my mind, I would be like Cinderella, and he would come and find me and we would live happily ever after. Because the real me wasn't "this type" of girl, I thought this is what *all* the girls did. In hindsight, I resembled a criminal who flees a crime scene when the cops show up.

My mum was the cop. I was the criminal. And I was seriously wondering if I could get arrested for this type of behavior.

I ran to her car and hopped in with a casual, "What's good, Mama?" I had never said those words before in my life; nor have I said them since. Apparently, kissing a boy turns you into a gangster. (Don't say I didn't warn you.) Shooting me back a clearly confused and suspicious look, she decided it would be safer for both of us if she didn't ask me any questions. For that, I was so grateful.

That night I couldn't sleep. I replayed the events over and over again and realized what an idiot I had been. I was so desperate to feel accepted and wanted, I acted like a different person to that boy, to my friends, and to my parents. None of the parts I played were the real me.

As for God, I don't think He was angry at me about the kiss. It took me a while to realize this, but now, thinking back on that moment, I imagine God watching me kiss that boy and thinking to Himself, "No . . . Elyse." The tone of that *no* is important. I don't think it was an angry no but a "that's not who you are" type of no.

God always saw the real me, even when I tried to hide it.

So . . . what did I learn?

When I think back on this story, I wish it could have ended differently. I wish I had walked away sooner. like writing a book, I wish I could just edit certain parts out. Unfortunately, life doesn't allow us to edit. But it does allow reflection. Here are a few things I learned from my experience.

> Unfortunately, life doesn't allow us to edit. But it does allow reflection.

1. Kissing a boy won't make you feel loved any more than fleeing a scene will make you look like Cinderella. Just FYI.

2. God will always see the real me. I might try to perform for my friends, or my parents, or even a boy, but God always sees, and He always knows. Sometimes I need to look to Him for a reminder.

3. If a boy can't love the real you—he doesn't love you.

Open Your Journal

If you've had a situation like mine, I pray in the future you might be able to pull some lessons from your experience like I have from mine. One good way to do this is to journal honestly through your thoughts in a place where no one else will read what you've written. This is the section where I ask you questions and you write the answers in your personal journal. This is your chance to say *exactly* what you want to say.

1. How many "you's" are there out in the world right now? Describe them. Are any of them the real "you"?

2. Ask the Holy Spirit to speak to you about who you are, and write down what He tells you.

3. Write down something you can tell yourself next time you're in a situation where you feel like acting outside your true self. Remind yourself that the real you is the best you, and visualize saying this to yourself next time you find yourself pressured to do something you don't want to do. Practice walking away. It starts in your head.

CHAPTER SEVEN

Drunk at a Wedding

HAVE YOU EVER been around people you wanted to impress, but instead you acted like a complete idiot? Did that group of people include celebrities and also your parents? No? Just me? Awesome!

Years ago, I was invited to a high-profile wedding. A friend of mine was marrying a pro football player, and the wedding promised to be full of celebrities, cameras, and other glamorous things. This was my chance to show my stuff and become channel seven's new weather girl . . . or something similar. Not that I cared.

The big day arrived with perfect summer weather, and I had the spray tan, outfit, and hair to match. I was so excited. This was the most exclusive event I had ever been to. The ceremony was intimate and simple, with only about fifty cameras poking and prodding the bridal party to get a good shot of the happy couple. (Okay, maybe not so intimate and simple. But it was special.)

As I arrived at the reception, I realized I had overlooked one small thing. I was still with my parents. If I was going to make any progress in the entertainment industry tonight, I was going to have to skip away from them and fast! I kept looking for my moment, but as it turned out, the bride had organized it for me. I was seated at the opposite end of the ballroom from them. With hundreds of guests, that was plenty of space for me to work the crowd and impress everyone.

I gave my mum and dad my best "disappointed" face, pretending to be sad that I couldn't sit with them, and juxtaposed it with the most fleeting good-bye kiss on record.

As I searched for Table 3, I imagined who might be seated next to me—Justin Bieber, Taylor Swift, Kim Kardashian . . . you know, the usual crowd. Okay, so maybe none of them were in attendance (or in the country), but my imagination was on overload! I felt like I was walking through the lunchtime cafeteria, looking for my table. And just like in high school, I knew the table I was invited to could make or break my night.

Then, I saw it . . . Table 3. If we had dramatic background music assisting with this story, it would come to an abrupt halt right here.

"Really? *That's* my table?"

Moving Tables

While I was grateful the bride had not put me at a table with my parents, I was offended she had put me at the table with the Socially Awkward Christians. To make matters worse, there were nine people at each table, which meant this table had four newlywed couples and me. Awesome. The night just went from party to pooper.

As I sat at the table pretending to listen to everyone's "funny" (the quotation marks were necessary) wedding stories, my eyes started wandering. Where were the cool kids? Where were the celebrities? Where was my clique? And then, like the heavens opening up with a Hallelujah chorus, I saw it—the table I'd been looking for all night. And it was right next to me . . . Table 2.

The best part was, I knew a girl at that table. Without even excusing myself from my own table, as if time were of the essence, I got up and sauntered my way over to Table 2. To my surprise (yet delight) the girl I knew jumped up and embraced me, demanding I pull up a chair.

"Well, if you insist," I smirked.

I had found exactly what I had come looking for—two TV personalities, two football players, and one Olympian swimmer. This was going to be a good night.

The Olympian introduced himself and immediately poured me a glass of champagne. That was the start of it . . . the first of many glasses. With each sip, a little more of me disappeared. With each glass drunk, I lost a little more control. I was no longer in a position to hold firm to what I believed or how I wanted to act. I had come to this table to impress these people, and in order to impress them, I had to act how they wanted me to act.

When it came time for wedding speeches, my table was rowdy. To say they were disruptive would have been an understatement. The boys were yelling loud, inappropriate comments throughout the speeches, and one even broke a glass as the groom was speaking. I was embarrassed and wanted to tell them to be quiet. But I couldn't. After all, I was one of them now, wasn't I? All I wanted was for them to like me.

To make matters more difficult, they kept filling my glass of champagne and encouraging me to keep up. I wasn't a big drinker. But who was I to refuse them?

As the night progressed I tried to remain conscious that my parents, although not close, were on the other side of the room. This task became more and more difficult. At one stage I thought I was in a great state to go over to them to "check in." I thought I might be able to convince them that I was doing great. From my point of view, I was smooth and subtle, holding on to every chair I passed and looking over people's heads instead of into their eyes until I reached my parents. Quickly realizing I wasn't as lucid as I first thought, I fled my parent's table before they could ask me any questions that required a thought-through response.

> Unfortunately, my desire to "fit in" cost me my convictions that night.

I felt accepted by Table 2. These people, whom society talked about, were talking to me. It wasn't *just* about Table 2 though. It was about being able to break into a group of people who didn't grow up in church. It was about reassuring myself that I was still "relevant" and cool enough to fit in anywhere I wanted. Unfortunately, my desire to "fit in" cost me my convictions that night. Deep down I knew these relationships would never last, but I had convinced myself I was one of them.

I convinced myself that was what I *really* wanted.

Time to Dance

The people at Table 2 stood up and rushed to the dance floor, but when I stood, I rushed back to my seat. I guess I hadn't realized how much I'd had to drink until I had to hold myself up—a nearly impossible task. Determined to keep up, I stumbled my way to the dance floor and insisted I *liked* dancing close to the floor. This was the latest move, I explained. It was all the rage in Hollywood.

Mr. Olympian picked me up and held me as I attempted to sway my hips, doing my best to convince everyone around me that I could keep up with them. I was in a bad way, and I had not thought this far ahead.

As Mr. Olympian walked me back to my seat to pour me another glass (as if I needed it), my parents arrived. Oh no. It was time to leave. After a quick pep talk to myself (probably loud enough for all to hear), I got up slowly and followed them out. I was moving at a tenth of their speed. Any faster and there would have been a collision with another oncoming guest or a chair. I was sure of it.

We walked out of the ballroom and into the parking lot. That's when things got really bad. I couldn't have kept my mask on if I had tried.

There's no delicate way to say what happened next. I puked my guts out. It was bad. Although my parents were clearly perplexed, they leaped into action. My mum took my purse and shoes while my dad held my hair back. He obviously drew the short straw. After what seemed an eternity, they moved me to the car and we started home.

For the next hour I lay with my head on my dad's lap as he held my hair and stroked my face. I doubt he had ever seen me in a worse state. I remember crying, "I'm so sorry" in between vomiting episodes. He simply whispered, "Shh. It's okay . . . I love you . . . it's going to be okay. Shh."

I could tell he had a million questions, but he knew that was not the time to ask them. What I needed at that moment was the comfort of my dad. I didn't need a group of people feeding my ego. I didn't need someone to give me a lecture about what I had done wrong. I already knew I had done something wrong, and I was suffering the consequences. What I needed was someone who would love me when I was completely unlovely. That night my dad was Jesus with skin on.

> What I needed was someone who would love me when I was completely unlovely.

I don't remember the rest of that night, but I woke up the next morning in my bed wearing my pajamas with my teddy bear tucked under my arm. My tongue felt like death, and my head was threatening to erupt like a volcano. There is no worse feeling in the world—I'm sure of it. I wanted to crawl into a hole and die.

I hobbled down the hall to my parents' room. Dad was quiet in a way that was unlike him, and I could tell he was disappointed and sad. I felt completely humiliated and yet completely safe. I crawled into their bed like I did when I was a little girl, because I felt like one again that morning

"I'm so sorry, Dad," I whispered in between tears.

"How are your new friends?" he asked and smirked a little.

I giggled and shook my head. "I won't be seeing them again anytime soon."

So . . . what did I learn?

Some lessons in life are harder to learn than others. All of our actions have consequences, but some consequences are bigger and heavier. This was one of those times when I knew I was forgiven for my actions, but I still had to bear the consequences for them.

This is one of the hardest things about being an adult. When you're a kid and you do something wrong, your parents punish you by putting you in the naughty corner. When you're an adult, there is no naughty corner. You get to make decisions for yourself, and you bear the consequences for yourself.

Here's what I learned from my experiences.

1. Everyone is trying to impress everyone, and none of it is that impressive. The people you're working hard to impress right now may not be there when you need them.

2. God will forgive everything, but He often allows us to experience the consequences of our actions, because perhaps it's time to grow up. Forgiveness is free, but sometimes we pay for our actions with consequences.

3. My dad taught me about the grace of God. Sometimes when we deserve a lecture, He holds our hair back and whispers, "I love you." It's the times we are completely humiliated that we are safe with Him.

Open Your Journal

If you've had a situation like mine, I pray in the future you might be able to pull some lessons from your experience like I have from mine. One good way to do this is to journal honestly through your thoughts in a place where no one else will read what you've written. This is the section where I ask you questions and you write the answers in your personal journal. This is your chance to say *exactly* what you want to say.

1. Describe a time (maybe you've never told anyone) where your desire to impress the people around you caused you to lose your convictions. If God's reaction wasn't anger, what do you think it was?

2. What are some of the consequences from that event? And what are some of the lessons you can take away?

3. Journal a conversation with God in which you imagine that He's holding your hair back and comforting you. Imagine He's the kind of God who tucks you into bed and tucks your teddy bear under your arm.

4. Read Romans 8:37–39 (in *The Message*, if you can) and write down what you think the Holy Spirit is saying to you.

Confession #5

I'm Controlled by Fear and Anxiety

'VE BEEN SCARED MY WHOLE LIFE. As a young girl, I was always afraid something bad was going to happen to me. The older I get, the less worried I become about outside forces, and the more worried I become that I might actually do something to ruin my life. I fear that I'm going to mess everything up; I'm going to fail. The more afraid and anxious I become, the more likely I am to fail or, even worse, remain stagnant. It's a self-fulfilling prophecy.

What I'm realizing is that fear and anxiety show me how much I'm relying on myself. When we rely on God, we don't have to worry about messing everything up. Even if we do (and we always do), He can fix it.

Fear and anxiety are exhausting, and they accomplish nothing. I'm learning how to put them down and how to break the cycle. Want to join me?

CHAPTER EIGHT

Night Terrors

IT WAS THE MIDDLE OF THE NIGHT—2:22 a.m. to be exact. It was late enough for everyone to be in bed but early enough that no one would be awake (except for me, of course). In my opinion, this was the perfect time for a thief to come into the house and steal my new straightener or cell phone . . . or my brother. Or worse, to steal *me*! For two years I woke up at that exact same time every single night. In the quiet of the house, it was so easy for my imagination to get away from me.

By this time, I had already decided what I would do (and what I wouldn't do) when the would-be burglar broke into the house. If I screamed for Mum, he might hear me and be angry that I'd spoiled his chance (of getting my straighter—thieves love straighteners). If I didn't scream, he might stumble across my room anyway, see me awake, and take me so I couldn't become a witness. I was left no choice but to silent scream. I couldn't afford to actually be heard, but if I screamed in my mind, maybe this mother's intuition thing I'd heard about would kick in and she would come to my room with a lightsaber. It was worth a try. So I counted. One . . . two . . . three . . .

Cue: silent scream.

Unfortunately, there was no mother. There was no lightsaber . . . just more creaking floorboards and suspicions of an intruder. Splendid! My heart rate just hit a personal best, and I was soaked in sweat.

Elyse, I thought to myself. *You have to get help. Call again. With sound this time!*

One . . . two . . . three . . .

"Mum!" I startled myself, screaming louder than I had even meant to. I waited for the intruder to come bursting into my room to collect me, but there was no movement. No mum. No intruder. Still no lightsaber.

Well, he knows I'm here now, I thought to myself. *Might as well just go for it.* So I screamed again. One . . . two . . . three . . .

"Mum!"

"Dad!"

No answer. (Seriously guys, I could've been killed by a stampede of elephants by now and no one would've stirred.) So I decided to try one last time, this time shouting their names in quick bursts, one right after the other. "Mum! Dad! Mum! Dad!"

I wasn't going to let up until they came.

Suddenly I heard the footsteps up my stairs. *Thud. Thud. Thud. Thud.* These were not the tiptoes of a little English mother coming to her daughter's rescue. I was doomed.

Brace yourself, I thought silently. *It's been a good life.* The door opened. And just as fast as my anxiety arrived it departed. Apparently these *were* the footsteps of a little English mother, one who was angry to have been awoken in the middle of the night . . . again . . . at exactly 2:22 a.m. It was the 659th night in a row! This had become my life.

After seeing thirty seconds of a horror movie by accident (a badly made horror movie at that), I had not slept through a single night in almost two years. Every night there were shadows and creaking floorboards and internal arguments, and, no matter how hard I tried to convince myself everything would be okay, this always ended with me calling out for my parents.

I worried I was the only one who struggled with fear like this.

Not only had *I* had enough, so had my parents. They hadn't had a full night's sleep for as long as I hadn't. Forced from their bed by an incessant, high-pitched, teenage "alarm clock" they had not set to this ungodly hour, they worked to convince me there was no reason to be afraid.

Called Out

The following morning would feel like *Groundhog Day*, as I crept down the once dark, frightening stairs to breakfast with the same embarrassment I had felt the morning before. Every morning I saw the exhaustion on my parents' faces, and every morning I knew I was to blame. "What happened last night?" my parents would ask, concerned. Every morning I met the same question with the same answer: I didn't know.

I didn't tell anyone outside of my family about my fears, and I begged my parents not to tell anyone either. I didn't want people to know, because I worried I was the only one who struggled with fear like this. I felt like such a baby. I felt so pathetic. And to make matters worse, I was the pastor's kid. Didn't I have enough faith in God to overcome fear?

So I put on my brave face and pretended everything was fine.

No one needed to know. And no one *would* know . . . except for the prophetic pastor who specialized in freedom ministry. And he had come to our church—perfect. He seemed a nice, friendly, older man with grey hair and a slightly longer-than-acceptable grey mustache. He looked like a jolly geography teacher I had once.

Halfway through a service at church, I had my hands lifted to the right degree and was singing the right lyrics in worship (like a good church kid) when I felt this man take my hand and lead me to the front for prayer. As he began to talk to me and ask questions, I knew this was going to be different from what I had experienced in the past. He wasted no time in asking me about my nightmares. I couldn't believe my parents had *told* him. But they hadn't.

He told me God wanted to get rid of my fear and replace it with peace and rest, and he prayed for me that night. There was nothing magical or forced about it. I didn't shake or laugh uncontrollably. It was just a quiet, firm prayer. I felt the unmistakable power and peace of God and remember wanting to stay in that moment of peace and overwhelming security forever. When we finished praying, I thanked him and returned to my seat.

I have never woken up at 2:22 a.m. since that prayer, which was thirteen years ago. The handful of times I have woken up in the middle of the night (always at a different time) I have been able to pray and go straight back to sleep. I've never had to yell for my parents again (I'm sure my parents are stoked, even if they won't admit it).

What I realized from this experience was that the only way I was able to overcome fear was to talk about it and let God deal with it. It was never my battle to fight anyway. As long as I kept fear in the dark, it felt too big for me to handle. Fear was so big it felt like it controlled me. But as soon as I shared my story, I realized I had what it took to conquer fear.

And so do you.

So . . . what did I learn?

I hate fear, although I don't know anyone who's a massive fan of it. The more I have told this story over the years, the more I have realized something: I'm not alone. So many other young people (and older for that matter) have horrible stories about night terrors, anxiety, and interrupted sleep.

Why? We are afraid.

But fear is not unconquerable. Here are some things I learned from my struggle with fear and anxiety.

1. The more fearful I become, the more dangerous I am to myself. The more I choose to trust God, the more dangerous I am to the Enemy.

2. The best thing I can do to fight fear is to confess my story to others.

3. Fear was never in God's plan. He never gave it to us, and He will gladly take it away from us.

4. When we call upon Jesus, it's no competition. Fear has to go. This isn't a tug-of-war with even odds. Jesus trumps fear, every time.

5. God defeats fear with three weapons—peace, love, and a sound mind. (You can read more about that in 2 Timothy 1:7.)

Open Your Journal

If you've had a situation like mine, I pray in the future you might be able to pull some lessons from your experience like I have from mine. One good way to do this is to journal honestly through your thoughts in a place where no one else will read what you've written. This is the section where I ask you questions and you write the answers in your personal journal. This is your chance to say *exactly* what you want to say.

1. What are you afraid of in your life? What's the worst thing that could happen? Write down your worst-case scenarios on one side of the page.

2. On the other side, write down how you think Jesus would answer your fears. Imagine that He is sitting next to you. What would He say? How would He respond?

3. Look up 2 Timothy 1:7 and reflect on the fact that the three things God gives us are greater than the fear you feel.

CHAPTER NINE

Terrorist Attacks

SOMETIMES WE'RE AFRAID of things that don't actually exist, but other times we're afraid of real things, things that have the ability to impact our lives, things we can't just wish away. It seems like the more days that pass, the more dangerous and scary our world becomes. The longer I'm on this earth, the more things there are for me to be afraid of.

I've heard of people who are afraid to have children because they worry about the world they will be born into.

I've heard of people who refuse to travel because there are obvious risks, no matter if you're traveling by car, boat, or plane.

I've heard of people who want to start a business but won't because of the unpredictability of the economic climate.

I've heard of people who are afraid to get married because the divorce rate keeps climbing and climbing.

We'd rather be lonely than heartbroken. We'd rather have a buffer in our savings account than take a risk. We'd rather pretend we don't like traveling than take a chance of never coming home again. People in our world are staying stagnant for fear of the "what if." And in some ways, I can totally understand.

Our fears are not imaginary.

A Very Real Fear

Mum woke me up on a seemingly normal Wednesday morning. When I heard her in my room, I figured I had slept through my alarm again and was about to get in trouble for making her drive me to school. My fears of being in trouble were laid to rest as soon as I heard her voice, which was quiet and calm but not calm in a controlled sense.

It was the kind of voice parents use when they are preparing you for bad news.

"Honey, come downstairs. There's something you should see on TV. It's big news."

The intrigue of the situation forced me out of bed, still half asleep, and I stumbled down into the lounge room. I had no idea what I was about to see.

My brother and sister had beaten me there and were glued to the TV—mouths open, hearts broken, and eyes full of questions.

For about a minute, I stood in silence behind them, watching repeated scenes of planes crashing into two identical tall buildings with smoke coming out of them, like something straight out of an action movie. The bottom of the TV was a constant stream of words, updated numbers, phone lines to call, and quotes from interviews. I was so confused.

"What's happening?" I asked in a hushed tone.

Mum explained how terrorists had hijacked four planes in America and had flown two of them into the largest towers in New York. A third plane had crashed into the Pentagon, and a fourth had been directed somewhere else but had been held back from its destination by the passengers. It had crashed into a field nearby. Being Australian, I had never seen the Twin Towers before—and now I would never see them. They had collapsed due to the impact of the planes.

There were thousands dead, and it was on every channel.

"The whole world is watching right now!" I'll never forget my mum saying that.

Viewing those images, I felt overwhelmed with fear. The fear felt like a

> Something terrible had happened, and fear was threatening to keep me from ever making a decision or taking a risk again.

straightjacket, tying me down and keeping me still. I couldn't move. I couldn't talk. I didn't know what to say or how to feel. Isn't this how fear works? It steals the real you and replaces it with someone you don't even recognize.

Something terrible had happened, and fear was threatening to keep me from ever making a decision or taking a risk again.

For the next half an hour we sat and watched footage of the towers burning and collapsing, partnered with updated news from reporters who were receiving the information at the same time we were. I remember one image of an African American lady with her face covered in white dust, trying to run but collapsing to her knees, face in her hands and wailing under the weight of grief. I felt my stomach drop. Tears burned behind my eyes as I felt the pain of a woman, just like me, whose world had crumbled around her.

The streets in New York were in absolute chaos and so was my mind. I had so many questions. Who would do this? Is it going to happen in Sydney? What's a terrorist? I honestly hadn't heard the word before.

And then, the scariest question of all: Where's Dad?

Never the Same

My dad traveled a lot, and we never really cared that much where he was in the world, just so long as he brought home presents at the end of a trip.

Suddenly, I cared.

Before my mind could predict that he was in New York and who knows what else, Mum explained that Dad was fine. He was stranded in an airport in Melbourne. All flights had been grounded until further notice. He was watching this unfold on a TV, just like we were. She assured me nothing bad was going to happen to him.

But how could I believe anything like that right now? This is how fear works. It takes over our ability to reason. I kept thinking about the father who I'm sure promised his daughter he would see her that night as he went off to work in the World Trade Center. Now he was never coming home again.

Everything is not fine! I thought to myself.

Although Mum acted confident in what she was saying, I could tell she was afraid, too. It's crazy how fear can make itself known even behind the most confident voice . . . even the voice of your parents.

Mum turned off the TV, and we began to get ready for school, in no rush. Getting to school on time didn't seem so important now. As I arrived, late to school, I went to get a late note, but the office lady told me not to worry and to go straight to class. I guess I was not the only one who had seen the news that morning.

I arrived to my class, one third of its usual size, to see a teacher who looked similar to my brother and sister that morning—reading the newspaper and playing a *Veggie Tales* DVD. Clearly this was not the day to be learning about algebra or metaphors.

I found a few of my friends, and before I could even sit down they asked, in unison, "Have you heard?"

Of course I had heard!

We spent the rest of that day in continuous discussion around the same subject. The whole day was a blur, and yet I can still close my eyes and transport myself back there as if it happened last week. It is hazy and yet crystal clear.

Fear does that to us.

That day, my world changed forever. My secure life was rocked to its core, and I suddenly had even more reason to be afraid than I ever had before. I was scared to grow up. I was scared to travel. I was scared to take responsibility in a world that was irresponsible. I was scared to take risks for what I loved and go after what I wanted. I was scared to lose the people I cared about most. I didn't want to be alone.

When I choose to say yes to God, even when I'm afraid, I discover the plan He has for my future.

And yet, somehow I knew this was the most important time for me to do all of those things—to love, to risk, to become the woman God had made me to be. This was the most important time for me to be brave and say yes to God.

When I choose to say yes to God even when I'm afraid, I discover the plan He has for my future. When I choose to stay with Him instead of running away, I become part of the solution, rather than part of the problem. When I choose to say yes to God I become part of a generation that will not shrink back and hide when turmoil comes, a generation that will stand on the front lines and take back what has been stolen.

This world is full of scary things, but we can't run for the barracks at the first sign of attack. We can't run away.

We must stand and fight.

So . . . what did I learn?

Maybe you don't remember September 11, 2001. Maybe you weren't even alive! But there have been moments since. Moments you do remember. Moments the world stopped and reminded us all that we live in a world full of scary things and imperfect people. So what do we do about it? Here are a few things I learned from my experience.

1. Replaying scary events over and over in your mind won't help you. Sometimes when fear seems to take over your life, or just your day, you need to learn to turn off your (literal or metaphorical) TV.

2. Even though the Enemy can cause horrible situations like terrorist attack on 9/11, I have the power in Jesus to stand up and chose to build my life upon the Rock. The Unshakable. The One who will never forsake me, who has already overcome the world.

3. It's important to remember and acknowledge (and even grieve) scary or sad events. This process is significant. But you get to decide when to move on, and the grief process might not take as long as you think.

4. I've read the end of the Book, and God wins. There's nothing to be scared of.

Open Your Journal

If you've had a situation like mine, I pray in the future you might be able to pull some lessons from your experience like I have from mine. One good way to do this is to journal honestly through your thoughts in a place where no one else will read what you've written. This is the section where I ask you questions and you write the answers in your personal journal. This is your chance to say *exactly* what you want to say.

1. Maybe you have a strong memory of something scary that happened to you, a time you messed up, or someone who really hurt you. Do you play the memory over and over again in your head? Write out the memory and then decide it's time to turn it off. You might tear the piece of paper into small pieces as a sign you're letting go of it for good.

2. If your fear is something you've never shared, or rarely share, who can help you process what you're feeling? Share your greatest fears with someone you trust. Everyone is afraid to share their fears, but when you bring fear into the light, it loses its power!

3. Look up John 16:33 (*Amplified Bible* if possible) and journal what you feel the Holy Spirit is saying to you about overcoming fear.

Confession #6

I'll Be Single Forever

MY LOVE LIFE (if I'm allowed to have a love life as a church kid) has for the most part been a giant flop. Don't get me wrong. There have been some big swells, moments of elation, just like in the movies, where if you were watching from the outside, you would think everything was about to fall into place. But then, always without warning, my love stories have taken a turn for the worse. I've been left standing confused and alone (in the rain . . . with sad music playing softly in the background . . . or something like that).

As if that weren't hard enough, I've watched my friends find their fairy-tale romances. And although I've been happy for them and proud of the guys they've met, I can't help but feel like I'm being left behind. Everything is changing. I don't know what's going to happen. And, if I'm really honest, I'm scared to love again.

The questions on my mind are ones I'd prefer never to say out loud: *Will I end up alone forever? Will I be able to handle the loneliness?*

CHAPTER TEN

Heartbreak Hotel

BEN HAD BEEN ONE OF MY BEST FRIENDS since the start of high school, and when it came to him, I had either been in the land of "giddiness and butterflies" or the land of "leave me alone; you're annoying." Ben felt the same. Back and forth, back and forth we went. He liked me, but I didn't like him. I liked him, but he didn't like me.

It was "one of *those*" friendships.

As we got into senior high, we joined the school performing band together. From there our friendship grew even more. Over the years, I would be lying if I said I hadn't put my first name with his last name somewhere in my daydreams (What? I'm a girl! It's what we do.) So it was clear to me (and to everyone around me) that I liked him. I just wasn't sure I wanted to act on it.

As for him, the older we became, the more certain he was he wanted to be with me. Unfortunately for him, I wasn't very good at the whole dating scene. I liked when he chased me but wasn't sure I wanted to be caught.

The excuse I always used when it came to dating was my dad. My dad had ten rules for dating his daughters before they were finished with school.

1. No.

2. See Number 1.

3. See Number 1.

4. See Number 1.

5. See Number 1.

6. See Number 1.

7. See Number 1.

8. See Number 1.

9. See Number 1.

10. See Number 1.

So when it came to dating Ben, I knew I always had an easy way out.

Somewhere toward the end of our back-and-forth flirtation, Ben auditioned for a nationwide, televised, talent show and made it through to the semi-finals. I was *so* proud of him and found myself suddenly feeling very protective of him. People started to recognize him (especially girls!), so although I was still hesitant to start a relationship, all of a sudden I felt the urge to call him mine. *Especially* when he announced he had a girlfriend. Talk about a plot twist. That was the final straw for me. It was becoming more and more clear I had to decide what I wanted. And I decided I wanted him.

After some encouragement (and miraculous approval) from my dad, and a hurry-up from my closest friends, the next week it all came to a head.

Indiscreetly, I texted him one school night and insisted he make sure I tell him the thing I needed to tell him during lunch the next day at school. We both knew what "the thing" was, but somehow "the thing" seemed more exciting if we kept it vague. I don't necessarily recommend telling a boy you like him if he already has a girlfriend. In fact, I highly discourage it.

But I was young and stupid . . . and deeply "in like" (or so I thought).

He Loves Me, He Loves Me Not

The next day at lunch, walking to sit with my friends, I felt sick. It must have been a mix of nerves, excitement, fear, and excess Diet Coke. I prayed he would forget all about my text message from the night before but just in case, I decided that if he came over to talk to me, I would pretend I didn't speak English and run away. Flawless plan.

But it was too late.

Before I could say, *"Je ne parle pas anglais,"* he was taking my hand and we were walking away from my group of girls, who were wolf whistling and screaming, "go get him, Elyse!" *Subtle, guys . . . really subtle.*

As we stood under the tree on the playground, we made small talk, both wondering if the other would bring up "the thing." I counted down from three in my head, psyching myself up to broach the subject, but he interrupted my thoughts by saying, "Oh, by the way, I'm single again." If this were a movie, this would be the place where everything would lurch to a stop and I would have a monologue to the camera. I would say, "What? This is great. And also terrible. Was I the reason for the break-up? Or did he want to be single? Was there someone else I didn't even know about? So many questions. So little time."

"I like you . . . a lot," I blurted out, before I could stop myself. (It sounded a lot smoother in my head.)

After what felt like a five-hour pause, he took a deep breath.

"I don't know what to say . . ."

Awesome. Let's just put this in an episode of "world's most awkward moments" and watch as it rakes up millions of hits on YouTube. I turned to walk/run away, to keep my red cheeks from getting any redder or my eyes from pouring the tears that had built up. But as the distance grew between us, he called out.

"Meet me in the music room after school!"

I nodded, dropped my head, and walked/ran away. I ran to the bathroom to phone (and *blame*) my friend Menae, who had recommended I tell him how I felt. She reminded me to relax and wait until after school. That's why best friends are, well, the best—they have a way of coming up with plausible excuses for heartbreaking reactions from boys.

The Music Room

After school I headed to the music room as nervous as a criminal about to hear her sentence from a judge. I entered the room, and Ben was sitting at the piano, playing music. When he saw me, he stopped and smiled.

"Come sit," he said and patted the seat next to him.

Honestly, I preferred to hear my rejections standing up. That helped with the speedy getaway, before my emotions could expose how much I liked him. I stood there silently, forgetting all social etiquette and rules of natural human interaction he spoke, and the verdict was handed down.

"The reason I didn't respond to what you said earlier today is because I was in shock. I've liked you for so long, Elyse. Of course I like you."

He liked me. He *liked* me. He . . . liked . . . *me*.

I tried not to be too obviously ecstatic, but I suspect the fact that my cheeks hurt from smiling and I couldn't stop giggling gave me away.

My birthday came a few weeks later, and he wrote me a song, singing it for me in that same music room. He would constantly send me text messages to reassure me how much he cared about me and was thankful I was his girlfriend. Every once in a while, especially at first, I would feel myself becoming afraid of commitment again and so would make up some ridiculous "rule" he had to follow in order to give me space. As pathetic as it was, he would quietly respect the rule and respect me.

The longer our relationship went on, the more I knew I trusted him.

After more auditions, he made it through to the "live rounds" of the TV talent show he was on. By now we couldn't go anywhere without him being recognized, which he found really difficult. I remember one Christian festival we went to where we walked about 100 meters the entire day, stopping every thirty seconds for him to sign autographs, take photos, and speak to fans.

The whole thing was bizarre. Neither of us knew how to respond.

The year intensified with my final exams, Ben performing every week at the live shows, and the speculation around our relationship growing. The stress this put on us individually and as a couple started to become overwhelming.

At first, when newspapers would write articles about him or radio stations would interview him, he would mention our "Special Friend" status. I thought it was so cute. But it didn't take long for things to become more intense.

I started receiving hurtful messages on the Internet from his fans, telling me I didn't deserve him, that *they* should be with him and that I wasn't good enough to be seen with him, let alone to date him. Within a matter of weeks I went from having 200 Myspace friends to over 10,000. At the shows I would put on a smile and a new dress, pose for photos, and even make friends with the crew. But behind the smile

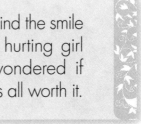

But behind the smile was a hurting girl who wondered if this was all worth it.

was a hurting girl who wondered if this was all worth it.

In the midst of all the fame, I wondered if this boy still noticed me.

Behind the Smile

The more fame he received, the more fragile our relationship became.

We found ourselves talking about the show all the time—about how he didn't want to be there and how he wished he had never entered it. My heart broke seeing him unhappy and insecure. This wasn't like him. He wasn't the guy I had come to know and trust. I found myself needing to reassure him constantly that I wasn't going anywhere. Our relationship was changing, and I wasn't sure I liked what it was becoming.

But I kept up the smile. As the cast shrunk from twelve down to three, we learned that he had made the grand finale.

My heart was torn. On the one hand, I wanted him to win, to live the dream of being an artist—that was what he had always wanted. On the other hand, I wanted him back. I wanted to be normal, again.

The grand final show came and went, and he finished runner up. Everyone assured him he would have a long career in the music industry, and he said he believed them. But it didn't make him smile. I hadn't seen him smile, *really smile*, in months. Once I finished my school exams, I told myself, things would go back to normal and we could finally go on that date he had promised.

But my final exams came and went, and the date never came.

I felt him pull away, and the harder he pulled, the harder I tried to hold on. I didn't want to let the first boy I really, truly cared about slip away.

One particular day, not too long after the show, I spent the whole day fending off questions from people at church. They asked about him and about us. I kept my smile intact as best I could, all day, not dropping the ball for a second. I reassured everyone he was doing great and would be back at church soon. I told them I had spoken with him that morning and he was missing everyone so much. I was lying.

> God, help me, I whispered, as I finally hopped into bed and cried myself to sleep.

I hadn't spoken to him for over a week and didn't even know where he was.

That night, after church, I was the first of my family to arrive home, and I went straight to my room. I took down my perfect hairstyle, changed out of my perfect clothes, wiped off my perfect makeup, and finally relaxed out of my perfect smile. With my pajamas on, a wave of emotion took hold of me. I collapsed to the floor and couldn't stop the sobs. I sat there for longer than I care to know under the weight of the pressure from the last six months. It was all too much.

God, help me, I whispered, as I finally hopped into bed and cried myself to sleep. I felt stuck, hopeless, and completely brokenhearted.

Something's Got to Give

As the next few days unfolded, I still didn't know what the future held for my life, but I knew God's plan for me was better than my current state of being. I spoke with Manae and finally confessed everything that had been going on.

She told me it was time to face reality.

Rather than give me an excuse for the heartbreak of a boy, she told me the truth, and I needed to hear it. This is the *other* reason to love best friends. I needed to let go—to let go of the boy I had known six months ago, let go of the idea of having a boyfriend, and let go of the nasty things people had said about me. I had known she was right. I needed her to remind me of what I already knew deep down.

The next day was our school presentation evening, which was a really big deal in our area. The school had hired out a massive entertainment center for the night, and Ben and I were supposed to sing together. I hadn't seen or spoken to him for two weeks (although supposedly we were still "together"). The first time I saw him was at rehearsal—in front of the entire school. Seeing him come toward me, I felt exactly as I had that day I told him I liked him for the first time. It was a mix of nerves, excitement, fear, and way too much Diet Coke.

In front of the whole school, he walked over, picked me up, and spun me round—just like a *High School Musical* moment. My heart melted, and I wanted to cry. I so desperately wanted to believe this guy standing in front of me was the guy I once knew, but he wasn't. I *knew* he wasn't. I whispered, "We *need* to talk."

Later, as we sat down to have a conversation, a sudden burst of pain hit me. Have you ever realized something you had such high hopes for was about to come to an end? This was that moment for me. And it hurt.

We talked and agreed that "taking a break" to concentrate on ourselves was the best thing to do. It wasn't a surprise to either of us.

He held my hand as we sat in silence for a few moments, and suddenly I was catapulted back to the music room, to the day he told me he liked me. Wasn't it only yesterday we were standing there with excitement at the start of this adventure? Or maybe it was light years away. Time stood still.

The year and its experience had changed us.

Walking out of that building at the end of the night after saying good-bye to him was both freeing and terrifying. I knew I'd done the right thing, but I couldn't help wish things had turned out differently. I wished they'd turned out like my dreams.

Long Road to Recovery

I wish I could say it was a quick recovery, that I woke the next morning with a spring in my step, ready to face the world. The truth is, I hurt for a long time. I spent far too long dreaming about what could've been. I wished he was still by my side. I cried myself to sleep and wondered how long it would take until he called me. I doubted my heart would mend and felt helpless at the thought no one would ever make me feel the way he did. Maybe you can relate. Heartbreaks . . . they physically hurt.

Yet I still remember the day I finally started to heal. It was at a youth summer camp, and I had no tears left to cry. I was exhausted both physically and emotionally. I had tried to move on but couldn't.

I was at the end of myself.

With the remaining strength I had left, my face hidden in my tear-drenched pillow, I whispered, "God, I can't do this anymore."

He said: *Let me.*

A wash of peace came over me, and for the first time since we'd broken up, I knew I would be okay. My God would look after me. I would get through this and come out stronger on the other side. He wasn't going to abandon me and leave me lonely.

So . . . what did I learn?

Have you ever had to see someone walk out of your life and know it was for the best but it broke your heart nonetheless? Have you ever been in such heartache that it literally made your *heart* ache? Have you ever broken up with someone you thought you would spend the rest of your life with? I hope you haven't, but part of me thinks you may know what I'm talking about. And you might be thinking of that person right now.

Here are a couple of things I learned from letting go.

1. Sometimes God needs to get rid of things from our lives to make room for even better things.

2. "Taking a break" from a relationship wasn't helpful for me. I spent too long after it was over wondering when we would get back together. The truth was, we were never going to get back together. (Thank you, Taylor Swift)

3. Keep looking forward. If the "best" days of your relationship are always in your past, it might not be a good relationship for you.

4. Keep your friends close. My friends were the ones who were there to support me and give me the advice I needed, even when I didn't want to hear it.

5. God has someone for me, even if I haven't found him yet.

Open Your Journal

If you've had a situation like mine, I pray in the future you might be able to pull some lessons from your experience like I have from mine. One good way to do this is to journal honestly through your thoughts in a place where no one else will read what you've written. This is the section where I ask you questions and you go write the answers in your personal journal. This is your chance to say *exactly* what you want to say.

1. How's your heart? Is there a reason it's hurting right now? Did you have to let go of something or someone you loved? Write about it.

2. Read Isaiah 54 (*The Message*) aloud to yourself. Fleur, a friend of mine, told me to read this passage during that tough season. I read it every day for three months. Through tears I would read. Through hopelessness I would read. Through anger I would read. Through confusion I would read. Through doubts of my future I would read. And now I want you to read and record what it says to you.

CHAPTER ELEVEN

27 Dresses

I'VE BEEN LUCKY ENOUGH to be a bridesmaid in five weddings. Four of them were in the space of six months.

I know. I'm still recovering.

When people discover this fun fact about me, the most common reaction is, "Wow, just like *27 Dresses!*" To which I reply, "Yep, I'm rivaling Katherine Heigl. I'm going for twenty-eight." Usually that gets me the smile I'm going for.

This rapid-fire wedding season was one of the most exciting and fun-filled of my life. I loved seeing my best friends step into a whole new world of adventure (*Aladdin*, anyone?) with its highs and lows and color schemes. Each wedding was completely different, but all of them involved people who played a significant role in my growing up. It's such a privilege to participate.

But with the preparations, dresses, parties, and debates about whether it should be a reception or a sit-down dinner came some moments of sadness. I had doubts and fears about my own special day. One person replied to my bridesmaid comment with a snide, "Always the bridesmaid, never the bride." As much as I pretended to laugh along with her (and practice self-control by not spilling my drink down her top), it stung inside, confirming my own secret fears. With each wedding, came a new set of reservations and questions.

Would I ever get to experience this?

Will I get married or forever be the bridesmaid?

The first two weddings were for two of the girls I grew up with in church. These girls have been best friends of mine since school, and we have the memories to prove it. (They're the ones who know my first kiss story and still like me.) They were my partners in crime, the girls I "ugly laughed" with. When a boy texted me, they were the girls

I would call to ask how long I should wait before replying. They were the girls I shared a cabin with at summer camp, the girls I would call when I was bored or lonely because I figured they were probably bored or lonely too!

We would arrive at parties together and even got a few joint invitations to those parties. (I'll admit, that part was kind of strange.)

So when the moment came for them to get engaged, I had mixed feelings. Everything would change now (as it was supposed to). They would now arrive at parties with their fiancés. Conversation would change from the planning of a girl's night out to the planning of a wedding. The stress of exams would become the stress of sorting out table seating. Anxiety moved from trying to impress a boy to trying to impress their in-laws. Life had changed.

With all the wedding talk, I began to have "wedding" questions. I wondered if I would ever get what they had or if I had missed out. Was this rapid-fire season the one shot I had to get married like the rest of my friends? After this season was over, would the opportunity be closed forever? It seemed like everyone I knew was getting married.

When would it be my turn?

The girls got married, and the days were magical. My friends each looked perfect. And the best part about being in a wedding party was I didn't have to worry about some weird, slightly-creepy-single-uncle asking me to dance. I had a bridal party partner!

The third wedding I was in was for my sister (who isn't *actually* my sister but may as well be). She lives in America, and we grew up as PKs together. We've been through the best and worst parts of church life together. She's the one I Skyped when I hated church people, and the one I vented to after a close family friend left the church. What would I have done without her?

When she got engaged, I was so excited.

She'd been dating her boyfriend for almost five years, and I had met him on several trips. He loved her completely, and I knew they were made for each other. So I knew it was time for them to get married (probably *past* time, if you asked me). Still, I wasn't sure if I was ready for the change I knew this would bring. My day-to-day interactions with her wouldn't change, but I knew something had shifted. It was time to become grown-ups. I just wasn't sure I was ready. I kind of liked the idea of a Peter Pan lifestyle, of only thinking good thoughts and flying to Never Never Land, where I didn't have to grow up.

To make the whole situation even more emotional, my friend and I had gone through everything around the same time. We'd experienced school, travel, and church together. We even looked like sisters. But now she was getting married. For the first time I couldn't say to her, "I know how you feel" or "I'm going through that too." This time I could only watch as my friend became a wife.

I walked down the aisle on her wedding day and looked around at the breathtaking setting. The ceremony was at a country club, the sun making a perfect shadow over the vintage arch at the end of aisle. Hanging from the arch were posies of white flowers. I hadn't seen many things in my life as beautiful as this. And she had designed it herself, of course.

As I watched her at the altar, the whole thing looked like a dream. She was a petite, blonde, innocent, angel standing there—promising herself to her husband, forever.

Did I miss out again? When will it be my turn?

I couldn't help it. The thoughts had crept in again, somewhere between bridesmaid duties and photo shoots. It was like they snuck up and pounced, arriving without invitation, the worst wedding guests ever.

I questioned God's timing. As I stood there, watching the bride and groom look into each other's eyes like characters in a sappy but stunning romance movie, I wondered: *When?*

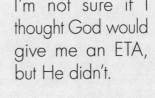

I'm not sure if I thought God would give me an ETA, but He didn't. Surprisingly.

I flew back to Australia a couple of days after that wedding, ready to be in my brother's wedding the very next weekend. (I told you it was crazy!) This was a big one for me. My brother . . . my big brother . . . the guy who had always faced the world with me . . . the one who protected me when boys would try to ask me out (or even when they just wanted to be my friend) . . . was getting married!

He was the brother every girl wished she had. And he was *my* big brother. I was his girl. And then he got engaged.

Now, he had *another* girl to spoil, *another* girl to focus on. Don't get me wrong, I couldn't have picked a better bride for him (I still claim I'm the one who set them up), and I was so proud to see him treat her as well as he had treated me. But I had to face reality. His wife wasn't going to move in with us so we could all live at home together.

He wasn't going to be coming home after work each day to hang out anymore.

When my brother got married, I would be the last child left at home. When I thought about that, the same old fears stirred up again. *Would I live at home forever? Would this last Murphy child find someone to spoil her, protect her, and love her, too?*

I'll never forget the moment I shared with my brother as I walked down the aisle before his bride. I turned the corner for the home stretch to the altar, and it was there I caught his eye. He looked at me and smiled, his smile hiding a thousand words. Behind that smile were memories of the twenty-three years we had spent together. There were the exact words I needed to hear—"You look beautiful"—hiding behind that smile. There was a "Thank you for looking after my bride" hiding behind that smile. And there was a reassurance that he would always be my big brother, my best friend.

I returned his smile with a silent "I love you" and blew him a kiss. And with that, it was time for his new chapter to begin.

As cliché as it sounds, I really didn't lose a brother that day. I gained a sister—a hilarious, crazy, loyal-until-the-cows-come-home sister. They are my best friends, my family. I want a marriage like theirs when I grow up.

So, do I have a favorite part of these weddings? That's easy. It's the same in every wedding.

It's the moment I wait for (just like Katherine Heigl), and it never disappoints. As the bride enters, from behind the trees, or at the back of the church, or at the top of the hill, I look at the groom. His face expresses everything my heart desires. The look of anticipation, love, and overwhelming confirmation that she looks far beyond anything he could have dreamed. With tears welling up or pouring over onto his cheeks you can tell that to him, there's only one person in the room—his bride.

In that moment I feel God whisper to me, *"That's how I feel when I see you."*

So for now, I'll wait. I'll keep doing what God has called me to do. I'll trust His ways are higher than mine. I'll remind myself that when the time comes, it won't be rushed, it won't be out of fear of missing out, and it won't be because it seems like the next "logical step" in life.

It will be because I found the person who makes my heart skip a beat and fills my tummy with butterflies. It will be because I have found the person who brings me closer to Jesus and cheers me on in the race I am running.

Oh, and bridesmaids? I hope you're ready to rewear your bridesmaid dress at my wedding.

Kidding . . . or am I?

So . . . what did I learn?

It can feel at times like weddings are contagious. (Thank goodness they're not. That could get awkward.) It feels like engagement announcements happen in batches. It's like everyone gets together and decides who will go first, second, third and so on—allowing just enough space in between announcements to give each couple "their time" but keeping it close together so everyone can experience it as a group.

Have you ever felt left out of that "group"? I know I have. Here are some things I've learned.

1. Sometimes waiting sucks. It was so hard for me to see everyone *else* achieve their dreams while I was still waiting for mine. I felt confused and disappointed.

2. Often I can get so caught up waiting for my life to begin (with a wedding or a certain job or finishing a degree) I forget to enjoy the moment I'm in. I heard someone once say, "Life isn't a destination; it's a journey." I'm slowly learning to enjoy the journey.

3. Remember to enjoy and celebrate others, even when they have something you want but don't have just yet.

4. The next time you're a bridesmaid, here are some things to remember. Take flat shoes to change into after the wedding. Have up-tempo music in the bride's room while she's getting ready. And do not under any circumstances let the bride hold anything that isn't white or clear near her dress. Trust me. I learned the hard way.

5. My time will come. God has promised me. And guess what—so will yours. He promised you too.

Open Your Journal

If you've had a situation like mine, I pray in the future you might be able to pull some lessons from your experience like I have from mine. One good way to do this is to journal honestly through your thoughts in a place where no one else will read what you've written. This is the section where I ask you questions and you write the answers in your personal journal. This is your chance to say *exactly* what you want to say.

1. Is there something you feel like everyone else is getting that you're still waiting for?

2. What could God be teaching you?

3. Read Proverbs 13:12 and Exodus 15:26. Is there something in your heart you need God to heal?

4. There is always a reason to say thank you. While you're waiting for what you want, what can you be thankful for? Write down three things and then thank God for them. It's amazing how gratitude turns our perspective around!

Confession #7:

I'm Not Pretty Enough

I KNOW PSALM 139. I've read it a thousand times. I'm a PK. I get that God loves me, knows how many hairs are on my head, and that He calls me His masterpiece. But sometimes I feel a little like the Mona Lisa—good-looking from afar, but far from good-looking. I know the theory, but when it comes to *feeling beautiful*, sometimes I'm just certain I don't measure up. In a world of filters, Photoshop, and Victoria's Secret models, how's a girl meant to define *beautiful*?

God looked at David's heart and said it was what was on the inside that counted, but we live in a world where that value isn't expressed. Does it *really* not matter what I look like? That can't be true. What I look like can dictate what job I get, what dates I get, and who wants to be my friend.

So where's the balance? Good question.

CHAPTER TWELVE

Mirror, Mirror

TO SAY I'M A FAN of Disney movies seems like a horrible understatement because, let's be real, I'm completely obsessed with them. I have a relentless, giddy love for them. I have a Pinterest page devoted to everything Disney and follow Disney quotes on Twitter, Facebook, and Instagram. And don't bother asking me to pick a favorite. That's like asking a mother to pick her favorite child. I *refuse*. Are you getting the picture yet? Obsessed.

I'm pretty sure my love for them is genetic. It must be. Not only were they an answer to prayer for my mum when I was growing up (giving her ninety minutes of precious peace and quiet), they were, more importantly, confirmation of what I had always believed to be true — life *should be* a musical! People are *meant* to break into spontaneous song, dance, and choreographed routines, mid-conversation . . . sometimes with complete strangers. I'm still trying to convince those around me this is true.

But take note: *It's going to happen.*

As I watched these movies, an amazing transformation would take place. I would become the princess. Seriously. (Don't pretend you didn't do it too . . . hey, I'm not judging. I'm impressed.) It didn't matter which princess was in the movie—Snow White, Belle, Cinderella, Jasmine, or Ariel. I so badly wanted to *be* them. After the movie I would wander around the house continuing my "role" as princess. It was a responsibility I took very seriously.

On numerous occasions I was caught brushing my hair with a fork, singing, "Wondering free . . . wish I could be . . . part of your world" or "A whole new world . . . a dazzling place I never knew." I would dance around on the lounge room carpet while dodging the sharp corners in the "Cave of Wonders."

I would often talk to my magic mirror: "Mirror, mirror on the wall, who's the fairest of them all?"

And a voice would come from inside my head: *Not you!*

This voice—this *monster* of a voice—crept in between sixth and seventh grade, and as I grew, so did the monster. It was subtle and sparing at first. But it grew meaner and more frequent. It seemed to wait in the dark of my mind, prepared to come out of its hiding spot at any moment of vulnerability. If I showed any sign of weakness or disappointment, the monster was ready to attack. I didn't invite it. Lord knows I didn't *want* it. But it was there. And I couldn't get rid of it.

I'm pretty sure this monster had a secret relationship with my "frenemies," because it seemed everything I would hear them whisper about me, or have them say to my face, was repeated by this monster. For four years the monster was relentless.

The monster changed me. I became increasingly more conscious of what I ate, took five hours longer to get ready for school (slight exaggeration), cut bangs in my hair to hide my ever-growing forehead, and created an "ozone layer" of perfume to disprove the incredibly creative and original "Smell-Lyse" nickname I had accumulated. In reality, it was a nickname that had lasted two months in elementary school, but as soon as the monster heard it, he made sure I never forgot.

One day I was sitting in my designated spot with my clique, talking about which Spice Girl I would rather be (obviously, I picked Baby Spice). I was sipping from my Diet Coke, the same "lunch" I had consumed every day for the last two years.

That's when I heard it, "Elyse, you've lost weight." It was our group leader and she was staring me down.

"Really? Me?" I tried my best poker face (unfortunately, being a church kid, I had never played Poker before).

I wasn't sure if she was accusing me or complimenting me, but either way I felt like I'd just won Australia's *Next Top Model*. The whole group agreed and proceeded to tell me how jealous they were of me, mostly, I'm assuming, because once the "leader" notices something, no one else dares disagree.

So at lunch, three of the others decided to follow suit and have a Diet Coke and nothing else. Copycats.

That was how the monster in my mind changed tactics. *See, the less you eat, the more beautiful you are. Just make sure no one gets skinnier than you or you'll lose your edge; skinny = happy.*

Losing Control

The coming years were full of trial and error. I tried almost everything in an attempt to maintain control over the monster in my mind, which was feeling more and more out of control by the week. I wasn't eating. And when I did eat, I would try not to let it stay down. I certainly had moments of hope during that time—ministry on an altar call, confiding in a trusted friend—but it never lasted. It wouldn't be long before I had a smile on my face, reassuring everyone that everything was going to be fine.

Inside I was screaming out for help. And sooner or later I would be back to my old antics, desperate to regain control over my body.

Of course, being a pastor's kid, I felt like I had to have it "all together." I couldn't be struggling with this issue. Not in public anyway. And so, while I was fighting with this, I was helping other girls, younger than me, deal with this very issue themselves. I was pretending I knew exactly how to win the fight. I knew all the right things to say; I just wasn't able to apply them to my own life.

The feelings of hypocrisy and guilt were overwhelming.

I can now see my parents would have embraced me with grace if I had told them. But as far as I was concerned at the time, discussing it with them was out of the question. Sundays came and went, and so did my smile and church-talk. I never reached out. And it was eating me up from the inside (pardon the pun).

To be honest, I can't pinpoint a moment when everything magically changed . . . when the monster in my mind disappeared. However, I *can* identify moments that helped me take a step in the right direction toward healing. The first, and perhaps most significant, was the day I finally confessed what I had been doing. Fleur was a really close friend of mine and a leader at church, who had been praying for me on this very issue for years. She led me to pour out my heart one day, judgment free. Fleur allowed me to release the built-up anxiety and secrets I never thought I'd be able to share. Fleur prayed with me that day and gave me Scriptures I hung up around my room to begin my plan of attack.

Once it was in the light, once I'd revealed the monster, he was exposed as the liar he was. And when the light switched on? I realized he was all talk. His shadow was so much bigger than his reality, and I couldn't believe I'd let that little thing taunt me for so long.

I can recall a moment I had with God where I physically felt a release from the need to be perfect, including the issues I had with my body. I also realized as I spoke with God about my broken identity that, while starving myself definitely wasn't healthy, it wasn't wrong to desire a strong and healthy body.

That day I called a personal trainer and nutritionist to give me practical advice to keep a balanced diet and healthy lifestyle, which included cutting down my crazy amounts of Diet Coke! As I write this, I'm realizing how far I've come. Now, by God's grace, I'm actually able to tell this story as a testimony to help others without even being a

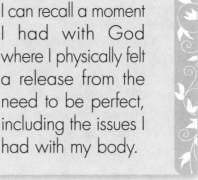

I can recall a moment I had with God where I physically felt a release from the need to be perfect, including the issues I had with my body.

hypocrite. I can be honest and open enough to say that the monster still attempts to come back from time to time, but now I have the tools in place to shut him down quicker than I ever thought possible. God has healed me, and He can heal you, too.

So . . . what did I learn?

This is an issue that affects all of us. I personally have *never* met a girl who hasn't struggled in some way with not feeling good enough, with wondering if her body meets the standard of the world. While my story isn't one of the worst you'll ever hear and it didn't end up where it could have, the early signs were there. And maybe they are there in your life too.

Here are some of the things I learned.

1. I need to do the best I can with what I have and trust God to do the rest.

2. I'm not as good of an actress as I think, and neither are you. The people who are asking questions love you and care about you. You can confide in them.

3. Starving yourself will never make you feel "good enough." There will always be things you want to change, things you wish were different. The only thing that will make you feel "good enough" is to shut up the monster. That will be the best feeling ever.

4. If you know someone who is struggling with an eating disorder, accusations (or flattery) won't help, but friendship and prayer will. You can be like my friend Fleur to someone in your life.

Open Your Journal

If you've had a situation like mine, I pray in the future you might be able to pull some lessons from your experience like I have from mine. One good way to do this is to journal honestly through your thoughts in a place where no one else will read what you've written. This is the section where I ask you questions and you write the answers in your personal journal. This is your chance to say *exactly* what you want to say.

1. Maybe you saw yourself in my story. What is the monster in your mind saying?

2. What is the next step you can take (maybe it's little, maybe it's big) that will start you on the journey to shut up the monster?

3. Find three Scriptures that speak to you (not just Psalm 139) about your beauty and self-worth, and hang them up in your room. Google is your friend for this.

Confession #8

I'm Lonely

I REMEMBER BEING AT SUMMER CAMP and scheming to be in a cabin with my best friends. You could tell they were my best friends because they were in my "Top 5" on Myspace. It was official. After the night meeting we would head back to our cabins and spend hours eating too much Cadbury chocolate, drinking too much hot chocolate (okay, fine, too much soda), and talking too long about our "camp crush." We would make plans for the rest of our lives and make promises to be each other's bridesmaids one day. And finally we would lose the fight to stay up all night. Many nights I would lie awake, staring up at the bunkbed and the feeling of loneliness would creep in. I was sleeping in a room with girls who knew me better than anyone, but did they actually *know* me? In a room full of my future bridesmaids, I felt isolated.

When is someone going to ask how I really am?

More importantly, when am I going to take the mask off and respond honestly? Because until I do, I will be lonely.

CHAPTER THIRTEEN
Mean Girls

'VE ALWAYS HAD A DESIRE to be loved, to feel accepted. I'm certain I'm not alone in that. As a church kid, I grew up feeling like I needed to be what everyone wanted me to be—a sweet, reserved girl modeling what a Christian daughter being raised up "in the way she should go" looked like. Unfortunately, there were a couple of issues with that. First, asking me to be a reserved, studious pastor's kid is like me asking you to lick your elbow. (You just tried, didn't you? It's nearly impossible, and the rare few who can accomplish it are kind of weird.) The second problem with me trying to be perfect was that I never felt like anyone *really* knew me, mainly because I never let anyone close enough to do so.

I honestly believed if people got to know me—the real me—they wouldn't like me.

Attempting to be sweet and reserved didn't cause too much grief in my early years at school. I went to a Christian school so everyone was a "church kid." Everyone was polite and well-mannered.

But it wasn't long before things changed. Drastically. At the start of grade five we had forty new students enter our grade, and more than half of these were girls. And they weren't church girls. These were girls who had come from public schools, girls who were determined to make their presence known and mark their territory early on.

I quickly realized that being a sweet, reserved Christian wasn't going to get me any friends. *Well, at least I can stop pretending I'm shy,* I thought to myself. As I watched the groups form around me, I worked out that I had two distinct groups to choose from: the Christian nerds or the cool mean girls.

If I had chosen the first group, this story probably wouldn't be in my book, so I'm guessing you can see where this is going.

Mean Girls

For the next two years, I worked my way into the second group. I learned to wear my hair a certain way and learned to say, "Hey, besties" with the right inflection. I even learned to get 70 percent on exams—this meant I wasn't an absolute idiot, and it meant I wouldn't get in trouble from my parents, but most importantly it meant I wasn't smart enough to be called a nerd and lose my spot in the group. I was even careful not to reveal my massive crush on Christopher Carter, because one of the other girls had decided she liked him first. I was left with Mitchell Dudley. Ew.

It wasn't long before I became so good at this act that I nearly had myself fooled. I was a little too good—smiling and hugging even when I wanted to scream and rip out my hair. I knew when to strategically place a "no offense" on the front of a comment, because apparently that made everything okay.

And I would never, *ever* let them see how dreadfully unhappy and insecure I had become.

I smiled. But I hated life. I was never at ease. How could I be with so much at stake? If I let my guard down for a second, I knew I would be out of the group faster than I could say, "Love ya, kiss kiss!"

For example, I remember going to sleep early at a sleepover party one night, only to wake up a few hours later with toothpaste in my hair and thick pen drawings on my face. I remember running and locking myself in the bathroom, unable to stifle the sobs coming from the pit of my stomach. I wanted my mum to come and save me but was determined not to give these girls that satisfaction.

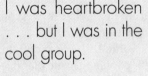

I was heartbroken . . . but I was in the cool group.

Sadly, this kind of bullying continued. Even worse, I wasn't always the victim. Sometimes I was part of the problem.

Finally, I decided it couldn't go on any further. I had to act, had to lead the revolution. I had to do something.

Time to Act

During an extra hot summer's afternoon at school, when Mr. Lucas had given up trying to get our attention, I was sitting with the group leader, Michelle, and her best friend, Laura. I was completely eavesdropping on their conversation while pretending to do my math worksheet, happy to be sitting at the same table as them. Michelle had been especially horrible toward me. She was the mastermind behind the sleepover incident and the reason why I wasn't allowed to wear my favorite-smelling LipSmacker anymore. (I wish I were joking.)

Michelle was telling Laura how she had gotten caught sneaking out of her house over the weekend. She needed Laura to check her email for her. I still remember the password Michelle conspicuously wrote out on a piece of paper and handed to Laura—iluvmatt. Shh, don't tell anyone.

And then it hit me. I could do a lot of "good" if I got into her email. I could prove what a mean girl she was. I couldn't wait to get home.

I ran home that afternoon and threw my oversized school bag on the ground, forfeiting my afternoon snack. "Ain't nobody got time for that, Mum!" I rushed to the computer and linked up to the Internet, the old-school, dial-up way. The computer buzzed and hissed and purred. Then I was online. Without really having a plan, I logged onto Michelle's email. To this day I still don't know how I devised this plan, it just kind of . . . happened.

Two hours later I had sent emails from Michelle's account to everyone in our group, including myself. I emailed myself, not only to prevent blame but also because I would prove to myself, in some weird way, that I really was in the cool group. Each email had comments that I knew would upset the recipient, mean enough so they would hold grudges against Michelle but not so horrible that they would confront her. Because everyone knows that in Girl World you don't confront; you gossip.

It worked. The next couple of days at school were intense, with people confiding in me they'd received these emails. I was in the power seat. And I liked the control. Of course I had convinced myself I was helping these girls, that I would lead them to church, that they could forgive Michelle and would become Christians.

"All things to all men," was my motto. Not only was I manipulating those around me, I knew how to manipulate the Bible verses I had heard on Sundays so that they made me feel better about my Mondays. Church-kid skillz—yes, the z was necessary.

After a while though, the news died down, and things returned to "normal." I was losing power. I needed to act again.

So I did. I sent a second, more vicious round of emails, hoping that the reaction would last longer. It certainly did. The next day as I got off the bus at school, I was confronted by the sight of angry parents lined up outside the principal's office, emails in hand, ready to have Michelle expelled . . . and possibly thrown in jail.

You could be in so much trouble, Elyse, I heard myself think. *No one can find out it was you.*

It didn't take long for our principal to realize someone had hacked Michelle's email, and she was determined to get to the bottom of it. Part of me suspects she may have watched one too many episodes of Sherlock Holmes, because she sprang into action, designing a chalkboard of theories, taking evidence, and conducting interviews.

Since I was a pastor's daughter, my interview with Mrs. Sherlock Holmes went something like this. "Take a seat, Elyse. Now, I know you didn't do this, and I'm almost embarrassed to ask, but did you send these emails?"

"Me? Seriously?" I responded.

"I know . . . I'm sorry I even asked. I know you didn't do it. You can go. Have a nice day."

Don't worry, Elyse. Technically you didn't lie, I reassured myself.

Except I *had* lied. To everyone around me.

To make matters *even* worse, the police got involved. Apparently the emails contained death threats! I had written, "Don't tell anyone I sent you this email . . . or else." In my mind, "or else" meant toothpaste in their hair . . . not death!

Taking Its Toll

It was all too much. I just wanted friends . . . real friends. I didn't mean for the prank to go this far. And the stress was taking its toll. I wasn't sleeping, and I wasn't eating. I certainly wasn't going near the computer.

My parents assumed my stress was because I was so affected by the emails I had received, because *I* was in the cool group. My family began writing me cards, sending me flowers, showing me extra attention. Their love and care only added to my stress and my shame. I couldn't take it anymore. *I was guilty!* Why couldn't I just tell someone?

Shame and guilt weigh a lot more on a teenager than skin and bone.

That week during a sports activity, I collapsed in the changing rooms.

Shame and guilt weigh a lot more on a teenager than skin and bone. As I recovered in the doctor's office, he explained I needed a few days off from school due to "stress leave." I didn't disagree, but this was a new low.

And with this new low came a reality check. I realized this was just the beginning. Even if I survived this fiasco without being exposed, I'd always know who sent those emails. I'd always know *I* was guilty. I'd always know *I* was the one who had caused such pain for my "friends."

I was the worst friend ever.

I felt so alone.

The Truth Will Set You Free

One of the best things my parents ever taught me was to listen to that still, small voice. They taught me to listen to the Holy Spirit. The entire time Sherlock Holmes was interviewing everyone and everyone else was sharing their own theories, a fight was going on inside me. On one side of the mental boxing ring were all the reasons I thought I shouldn't confess:

I hadn't done anything too bad.

It was better to keep this to myself.

They deserved it. I was merely doing what needed to be done. I was a sacrificial lamb, if you will.

On the other side of the boxing ring, there was only one Voice. It was small and still. It was relentless. I know now that it was the Holy Spirit speaking to me:

The truth will set you free. The truth will set you free. The truth will set you free. The truth will set you free.

I wanted to tell the truth so badly. I wanted to be free so badly. I knew if I could just confess to someone, if I could let out everything I'd built up inside, this weight would slide off my shoulders, and I would be free again.

As my mum was driving me home a couple of days later, I felt an opportunity. There was silence in the car, and I felt the Holy Spirit saying, *Now is the time.*

I opened my mouth, still not quite sure what would come out. My voice was hoarse and shaky.

"Mum, I know who sent those emails."

Before I'd even finished the sentence, tears were streaming down my face and falling into my lap. Mum stared straight ahead and was silent for a long time. The only thing that moved was her grip on the steering wheel. It got tighter as if she were unconsciously bracing for what she knew was coming.

Finally, she calmly probed, "Elyse, did you send those emails?"

Her question broke down the wall that had been holding back my ugly cry—the wall that had kept everyone else out and kept me in. I couldn't keep up the wall any longer. My tears and sobs were enough to give her the answer she'd dreaded.

When we arrived home, there was no lecture (although that was to come), and there was no punishment (although that was to come, too). When we got home, there was a moment . . . and I will never forget that moment.

Mum took my hand and guided me to the couch. She lifted me up on her lap like she had when I was a little girl. She looked me in the eye and told me she loved me. Then she led me through a prayer of repentance. And I've never forgotten that.

There were so many things that needed to be done, but being forgiven and learning the power of repentance was the most important. And I didn't have to do it alone.

I was free.

Too Late to Apologize?

The next twenty-four hours were full of phone calls and personal visits as I apologized to everyone I had emailed.

It wasn't an easy fix. I wish I could tell you that everyone forgave me instantly and it broke down the friendship cliques once and for all. But that isn't what happened. Far from it, actually.

As I walked into the classroom late the following Monday, everyone was already in their seats, and everyone had already found out I was the one to blame.

And that's when it happened.

Have you ever walked up to a group of people and realized they were just talking about you? Have you ever had it happen sixty times in a row? I have.

The rest of the year was *not* fun. As a young teenager, it was as close to hell as I could comprehend. I've never been bullied as much in my whole life. No one physically hurt me, but some days I wished they had. It would have been easier.

I begged my parents to let me change schools, but they wouldn't let me. And looking back, I understand why. Sometimes you have to stick it out in the storm. I couldn't see it at the time, but I'm so glad I did stick it out. Out of it came some of the best stories of reconciled friendships ever.

I am so glad I didn't run away. If I had run, I would have never seen the transformation in some of those girls' lives. Sure, some stayed the same, with their hair a certain way and their power-trips toward those less confident than themselves. But as time went on, others became close friends to me.

Actual friends. Real friends.

So . . . what did I learn?

The freedom I experienced when I became accountable is indescribable. I went from feeling completely alone to being free and full. It didn't mean cleaning up the mess was easy, but I didn't have to do it alone anymore. If you're facing a situation similar to this right now—it may not be the computer hacking type (although it might be!)—let me encourage you to tell someone. Maybe you went too far with your boyfriend or girlfriend, drank too much at a party, or got involved in something you knew you shouldn't. Maybe your situation hasn't escalated too far yet, but you know it could.

I learned some important lessons that year:

1. Just be nice to people. It's not that hard.

2. Saying "no offense" doesn't void a hurtful comment. No offense.

3. Secrets suck.

4. Listening and obeying the Holy Spirit is always smart. He's always right.

Open Your Journal

If you've had a situation like mine, I pray in the future you might be able to pull some lessons from your experience like I have from mine. One good way to do this is to journal honestly through your thoughts in a place where no one else will read what you've written. This is the section where I ask you questions and you write the answers in your personal journal. This is your chance to say *exactly* what you want to say.

1. Is there something you need to confess? Maybe it's something you've been feeling for a while or maybe it's something that has happened in the last few days. Ask the Holy Spirit and then be brave enough to write it down.

2. Lies will steal your freedom. Read John 8:32. What is the Holy Spirit saying to you?

3. Perhaps the thing you wrote down is something you feel challenged to confess to someone. The best thing you can do right now is put this book down, pick up your phone, and call your leader or a trusted friend and tell them. Trust me. In five minutes, you'll feel the freedom I've been talking about. It's time to be set free.

Confession #9

I Don't Have a Plan B

HAVING A PLAN B IS SAFE. Having a plan B is smart. Unfortunately, I hate playing it safe, and I've never been a genius. If plan A doesn't work, I don't want to have a plan B. Is that wrong?

Why do I need a plan B? You can only live one plan. Why not make it the one your heart desires more than anything? But with no plan B, you can be terrified of what will happen if plan A fails. This may sound like a complicated math equation, and I guess it kind of is, but here's what I'm getting at:

I'm very scared of failing.

CHAPTER FOURTEEN

When I Grow Up

THE WAY I SAW IT, I had three options. Depending on what mood I was in, there were only three ways my life would turn out.

I'm confident the first option is mirrored in every little girl's mind. Someday I was going to be a beautiful actress on Broadway. Unlike other actresses, I would accept only one role—Disney princess. Under no circumstances would I play the role of a villain . . . or a brunette.

If I wasn't feeling the Broadway vibes, I would move on to my second option. Judge Judy. Please tell me you know who she is. If you don't know who she is, Google her. Right now. She combines my need for justice and my love for drama . . . all in half an hour.

And no one—I mean no one—talks back to Judge Judy.

There were two slight hurdles to overcome before I could become Judge Judy, and my brother loved to remind me of them. The first thing I would have to do was to go to university for about 1,000 years. Apparently that's the only way to become a judge, even though I argued that it was just television. The second thing I would have to do was to change my name to Judy. That was a problem. I was growing pretty fond of my current name.

After a while it became clear that perhaps I only liked the idea of having control over others and being on TV. And I liked the idea of having a hammer, or a "gavel" if you want to get technical.

Don't judge. Pardon the pun.

If I couldn't get in the spotlight on Broadway or TV, I still had a third option. I would be famous.

Oh, how great life was going to be when I grew up! I would have a butler named Cadbury and an indoor McDonald's in my mansion. I would have a giant slide from my bed to my pool and an amusement park right outside with new roller coasters every month so I wouldn't get bored. Thank you for being my inspiration, *Richie Rich.* (If you were a child of the nineties, you'll understand.)

During these daydreams, I would lose myself in my own imagination and the possibility of what was to come. My dreams were frequent and time-consuming. And they seemed so possible and real.

I can remember one drive home from my grandparents' house, about a two-hour drive away. The night before, we had a guest at church who was on a popular Australian soap opera. Better than that, he was the young heartthrob on the show.

During the service that night, Dad decided to have our church pray together while holding hands. He asked us to look around and make sure we were all holding hands to represent our connection as a church family. Conveniently, I noticed my heartthrob (or, sorry the *soap opera's* heartthrob . . . my bad) wasn't holding anyone's hand. Being the sacrificial PK, I decided I should go and hold his hand. *We wouldn't want him to feel left out, now would we?*

I let go of my friend's hand and ran over to him, just in case anyone else had the same idea as me and beat me to it.

I got there first. Praise the Lord.

That brief encounter sparked my imagination. *I knew someone in the industry.* I could be in *the* industry. (Yes, you can laugh at me. I'm laughing at myself).

On the drive home from my grandparents' house, I got lost in my own imagination (again), dreaming what role I would play on the soap opera, which awards I would win at the Logies (Australia's version of the Oscars), and of course what dress I would wear and what cute guy would walk with me down the red carpet. We would cause the paparazzi to go into overdrive. Clearly, I didn't need much inspiration to get lost in the world of what could be.

It wasn't until we were just around the corner from my house that someone interrupted my "career plans" to make sure I was okay. Apparently I had been silent the entire trip but had developed a ridiculous smile on my face.

I guess I needed to work on my acting skills.

Feeling Special

For as long as I can remember, I felt special—and not just because my mum told me I was. I felt different from the people around me, like there was more to my life than anyone could see just yet. I felt it, deep down.

Maybe I got the "famous" thing a little off-center, and maybe I let myself watch *Richie Rich* a few too many times. Despite all that, I knew I was going to leave a mark on the world.

> Each one of us was created with intentionality and purpose. We were put here for a reason.

Maybe you've had these moments, too. Maybe they've been separated by feeling completely insignificant, but when you really have a chance to get quiet with yourself, you know you matter. You know you were put here with a purpose. And I feel pretty confident in saying we're *supposed* to feel this way. Each one of us was created with intentionality and purpose. We were put here for a reason.

That was me. I didn't know how, I didn't know when, but I knew I would do something that mattered someday.

Fame Isn't What I Thought

As I went through high school, I started seeing small signs of my dream becoming reality. I got some major awards for public speaking and scored some of the best roles in musicals at both church and school. I became one of the lead singers for our school's performing band, and my grades in drama and music were at the top.

Here's the truth: being onstage felt right. I loved it. When people spoke about staying behind-the-scenes or out of the way of the spotlight, I couldn't relate to them. I was happy for them, but for me, I absolutely *loved* being onstage, in the spotlight.

And yet, while I treasured those moments onstage, it wasn't long before I realized something. It was all so fleeting.

In the moment, being in the spotlight was exhilarating, with adrenalin pumping through me as I wondered if I could remember all my lines or if I was going to make the next costume change. And the applause from the audience (mainly my rent-a-crowd family) topped it off. I loved the feeling of being good at something. Who doesn't? But when the night was over, I would go home, wipe the makeup off, and crawl into bed. Long after the people had left, I would begin to dream again. Not about fame or acting or changing my name to Judy, either.

I would dream about preaching, about writing a book for young people, about traveling and leading people to know my friend Jesus. I dreamed about *significance*. It wasn't about making myself significant but about the part I could play in making God significant. I remember days I would go down to the beach, pull out my notebook, and write. I would begin to write about all the things I was going to do when I "grew up." I would write about the sermons I would preach, the places I would go, and the kinds of people I wanted to meet. Maybe you've done the same.

I would dream about what it would take for me to play my role in the bigger production that was taking place. I would wonder how long it would be until I could begin playing this part, frustrated that I was "too young" to start. I look back on those moments of frustration and wish I could have told my sixteen-year-old self what I feel now.

Growing up didn't start when I left my teenage years. Being a part of God's story has no discrimination of age.

Being a part of God's story has no discrimination of age.

I could make a difference then just as much as I can make a difference now or twenty years from now.

Significance is significance. We only find significance when we find our role in the greater story that is being written. And it looks different for everyone.

Maybe for you it's not about preaching or being on a church staff. Maybe it is. Maybe your significance is representing your country in sport (mine certainly wasn't) or being a high-profile lawyer bringing justice on the earth. Maybe your significance really is being a famous actor and in the spotlight, to have a wider platform to share the love and grace of Jesus.

Whatever significance looks like practically, I discovered one thing. I discovered significance would last longer than the lights and would still be there after the curtain had been drawn closed.

So . . . what did I learn?

I know something about you. Yes, you.

In your life you've had a moment, a thought, a whisper in your heart telling you that you were born for something more. How do I know? Because I had it, too.

Beyond the desire to be noticed, deeper than the ambition to be famous, I had a yearning to be significant. I still do.

Here are some things I've learned as I've processed—and am still processing—how that looks:

1. Life doesn't begin when I "grow up." Life has already begun; I'm standing in it. Significance starts now.

2. Knowing what I was born for lines up with my passions and desires. God doesn't give me desires that are opposite to my calling.

3. I need to protect my dream, to protect my plan A.

4. Dream big. That's the only way we're going to reach this generation.

Open Your Journal

If you've had a situation like mine, I pray in the future you might be able to pull some lessons from your experience like I have from mine. One good way to do this is to journal honestly through your thoughts in a place where no one else will read what you've written. This is the section where I ask you questions and you write the answers in your personal journal. This is your chance to say *exactly* what you want to say.

1. Write down three things that make you happy, three things that make you mad, and three things that make you sad.

2. Write down three things you are really good at. Don't skip past this one. It's important!

3. Could the things that make you mad, sad, and glad relate to the things you are good at when it comes to your dream?

4. Read Isaiah 55:8-9 and journal about how God's ways could be higher than the things you dream about.

5. Write out your dream. Write it out as big and scary as possible. You can do it. I dare you.

Confession #10

It's Hard to Tell the Truth

SEVERAL TIMES IN THIS BOOK I've urged you to uncover secrets—to tell someone your fears, to confess those things that have been hiding in the darkness. I know it's hard. Trust me, I really do know. It's hard to tell the truth.

But there's a very good reason I'm urging you in this direction.

I believe one of the biggest ways the Enemy will rip off our generation is by convincing us to keep things in the dark. Why? He knows he has authority wherever there is darkness. His power thrives in darkness. Where there is no light, he has full authority.

Where there is full light, he has *no* authority.

He's exposed wherever there is light.

Imagine a world where the Enemy has no authority. That is the kingdom of heaven, the one Jesus describes where the meek are blessed, where peace is kept, and where no one feels left out or lonely. It's possible to begin experiencing this world *right now*. It's possible to drag the realities of heaven into your experience on earth.

So I know telling the truth is hard. But I also know it's worth it . . . every time.

Will you join me as I learn to tell the truth?

CHAPTER 15

Life in the Fast Lane

CONFESSION: I'M NOT A GREAT DRIVER. No, really. I won't be winning the award for world's best driver or safest citizen on the road any time soon. But what a boring award to win anyway. Who wants *that* award? And yet driving isn't something I'll ever include on my resume under major skills.

One of the main reasons for my lack of expertise in this area would have to be the fact that I have the attention span of approximately ten seconds. After about ten seconds of concentration . . .

What were we talking about? I feel like a Diet Coke.

You can probably imagine how this causes some issues if I'm driving in traffic or am in a hurry to get somewhere. One minute I'm thinking about the stoplight . . . the next . . . who knows. And there was definitely a time, just after I received my driver's license, when my tendency to get distracted threatened to steal my driving privileges from me forever.

The plan was for me to drive home after a weekend away with the girls. We had stayed in a beautiful, beach holiday house about two hours north of Sydney. We had carpooled to the house, but I had to go home earlier than everyone else because I had to return to work the next day. This simply meant I would be driving home with nothing but my iPod and my thoughts to keep me company.

My parents were on a ministry trip in America, which meant I would have the car and the house all to myself. But as my sisters in Destiny's Child say:

All the women
Who are independent,
Throw your hands up at me!

We were having the best time doing all the typical girl things—attempting to surf, counting the freckles that were forming, and comparing our growing suntans. We were basically very busy, and the time was flying. On my final day, I explained to the girls that leaving early in the evening would allow me to get home without rushing and would prevent any tiredness at the wheel, especially since I was driving by myself.

Like I said, that was the *plan*.

We cooked dinner while blasting Beyoncé, each of us transforming into our own versions of "Sasha Fierce." Then a heated game of cards broke out, which led into karaoke (don't ask how), and before I knew it, it was time to go. Except I didn't want to leave.

You know when your alarm goes off in the morning and you roll over to hit the snooze button while promising yourself, "Just ten more minutes"?

That was exactly what I did, about twenty times.

Finally, I looked at my clocked and felt my stomach sink. "It's midnight! I gotta get home!" I squealed.

Suddenly, I turned into an evicted housemate on *Big Brother* and had only thirty seconds to gather my possessions. I threw everything that looked remotely like mine into my luggage, loaded the car, and wondered silently why I had brought three suitcases for an overnight stay.

After saying my goodbyes, in a way that suggested this was the last time I would ever see them again, I drove away.

With Taylor Swift good-byes my fists pumping, and my windows down, I was on my way home. I was happy.

I checked my GPS and it showed an estimated time of arrival of 2:20 a.m.

Now I have to confess (while I'm still confessing) that there's something about beating the time on the ETA of a GPS that makes me feel very accomplished, like I just proved a scientific theory wrong. I'm not recommending it, by any means, but I'm guessing you know what I'm talking about.

I calculated the driving time I still had left (another clear sign that I was bored).

"*One hour and forty minutes?*" I thought, "*Maybe for a bicycle rider!*"

I turned onto the highway, except this highway was more of a long country road with pure darkness at the end. There was no finish line in sight, just a few hills to keep you engaged along the way.

I took one last look at the GPS, dared it to stop me, and when it didn't, I put my foot on the accelerator. As my foot lowered, I watched the speed dial lift.

And lift.

And lift.

Suddenly, my car transformed into a vehicle in *Mario Kart*. I was dodging banana peels and using the mushrooms to give me extra speed. Don't worry. I was well aware of the red shells that could be flung at me! Unfortunately, I was under the false impression that my car had received a "star" from the magic item box and I was invincible from attack, and that if anyone came anywhere near me, they would get flung out of my way.

And they say kids these days spend too much time on technology. Whatever.

I watched as the GPS constantly updated. The more it changed my ETA, the more satisfied I felt, and the more my sense of judgment was silenced. *I was winning.* I wasn't sure what game I was playing, but *I was winning.*

I let out involuntary laughs that resembled something of Cruella De Vil. There was no way to stop them but, fortunately, no one could hear them! I had gone mad, and the adrenalin rush definitely didn't leave any room for remorse. After all, I had a time to beat!

Every now and then I would see a car up ahead and slow down until I had passed it. As soon as it disappeared into the darkness behind me, I put pedal to the metal again.

Let's just say I got home *well* before 2 a.m.

As I came to a stop in my driveway, I looked at the GPS. A big, defiant, smirk spread across my mouth and I took my hands off the steering wheel.

Without much thought, I set my alarm for the next morning and got ready for bed. After about half an hour of fidgeting, I realized why I couldn't settle down. My heart rate was sky-high. I tried breathing deeply and counting kangaroos (that's how we do it in Australia). I even tried a technique my mum had taught me when I was little, tensing all my muscles before relaxing them one by one.

I tried everything to get my adrenaline and heart rate to calm down. Finally, I stopped counting kangaroos and drifted off to sleep.

Reality Check

I sat straight up in bed, sweating and panting, my body overheating and my mind racing. I couldn't have been asleep more than a few hours. I had no idea what was happening to my body, but I knew it was bad.

Every image I'd ever seen of car crashes on the news came flooding back in a graphic PowerPoint presentation in my mind. The images were accompanied by a soundtrack straight out of a horror movie. The more I tried to calm down, the more panicked I became. I was having a panic attack.

Suddenly, involuntarily, I blurted out, "I could have *died!*" I had risked my life for something so trivial. There's competitive . . . and then there's just plain stupid. I had been the *latter*.

I sat there, staring into the blackness, traumatized.

After a few moments of trying to calm my breathing, my heart rate slowed. I attempted to bring my thoughts into some cohesive pattern. I was unsuccessful.

Reality hit me hard. I didn't deserve to drive my mom's car. I had been foolish and had put my life on the line. I had been an absolute idiot.

I didn't know what to do, so I started to pray—the thing to do when you don't know what to do, as any church kid will tell you. Let's just say it wasn't my finest prayer. It was a blubbering, nonsensical mess, but it was all I could muster. I asked God to forgive me for doing something so selfish. I thanked Him for being my star of protection, even when I was the furthest from deserving it.

> I didn't know what to do, so I started to pray—the thing to do when you don't know what to do, as any church kid will tell you.

I clearly felt God speak to me, and I didn't like what He had to say.

He told me I needed to call my parents in America and tell them what had happened. I needed to tell them the truth and ask for their forgiveness.

A million reasons why it was a stupid idea to call them flooded my mind. But then (and I think it was God), I was reminded that I had already *been* stupid. Why stop now? Touché.

I knew I wouldn't be able to sleep until I came clean with my parents.

With a heart full of regret, I fumbled around my floor for my phone.

I found it straight away. I dialed the number and prayed they wouldn't pick up. "Hello?" Mum answered on the first ring.

I guess that prayer was never going to work.

"Hello mother dearest, I hope you're well. Just thought I would give you a quick call to see how your trip was going and let you know of a small blunder I made today."

That's how I saw this conversation going in my head anyway. I took a deep breath with every intention to tell them calmly what had happened and how sorry I was. Reality? I opened my mouth and this is what came out.

"I'm *sooooooo* sorrrrry!!!" (This was said between sobs, heaves, and choking on my own tongue.)

I guess I didn't even realize how sorry I was. Through cries, staggered breaths, and broken English, I came clean.

Now I really was sorry.

My parents met my confession with grace, forgiveness, and the dreaded, "Let's talk about this again when we get home." I knew what that meant, but in that moment I didn't care.

As soon as I got off the phone, I lay down and went straight to sleep. For the remainder of that night, I slept soundly.

When my parents arrived home a couple of weeks later, we *did* talk about it. I *was* grounded from using the car for an eternity (or so it felt). But I wouldn't have had it any other way.

I had learned my lesson. Telling the truth is *always* worth it . . . always.

So . . . what did I learn?

When we bring into light what the Enemy tries to convince us to keep in the dark, we win. Period. I've had countless situations in my life (some more severe than others) where I thought the best thing to do was to keep something a secret. Some of those situations are now in this book. Take *that*, Enemy. So many times I've been scared to confess the truth, terrified of the consequences. I've learned a couple of very important lessons:

1. Beating a GPS is a stupid reason to speed and risk my life. I won't do it again. And don't you dare try it either.

2. Keeping things in the dark will only make the situation worse and cause me stress and anxiety. There is *nothing* more precious than the moment of confession. The freedom is unlike anything else.

3. I was forgiven once I confessed my sin to God, but it didn't take away my anxiety or guilt. When I obeyed the Holy Spirit and confessed my sin to my parents, that's when I was healed and free.

Open Your Journal

If you've had a situation like mine, I pray in the future you
might be able to pull some lessons from your experience
like I have from mine. One good way to do this is to
journal honestly through your thoughts in a place where
no one else will read what you've written. This is the
section where I ask you questions and you write the
answers in your personal journal. This is your chance to say
exactly what you want to say

1. Is there something right now that you are too scared to
   confess? Write it in your journal.

2. Ask God for forgiveness for *that* thing and thank God that
   when we confess our sins to Him, we receive forgiveness.

3. Read James 5:16 and reflect on the fact that when we
   confess our sins to one another, we get healing.

An Honest Confession Is a Good Confession

AS A GENERATION, we are obsessed with secrets and confessions. You know I'm right. We may not use it as a conversation icebreaker—in fact I would recommend you don't—but we are infatuated with them.

Like we did at the beginning of this book, let's look at the world around us. Everyone roots for the quirky investigator whose job is to work out if someone is lying so he can save the little girl kidnapped in an abandoned warehouse and rescue her stuffed bunny that's tied up next to her. And don't pretend you weren't glued to your television as the final episode revealed *who* Gossip Girl actually was (xoxo).

Closer to home, we can't help but investigate what *really* happened behind the breakup of that cute couple, even if we say it is to pray for them. We take on the responsibility of "private investigator" when we get that icky feeling after meeting someone new, convinced they're hiding some deep, dark secret we need to know.

Whether it's on the television, in a magazine, or in the immediate world around us, these things suck us in *every time*. Why?

Because we're obsessed with confessions.

Yes, but why? Maybe, just maybe, for a moment, uncovering someone else's confession allows us to forget that we have secrets of our own that need to be uncovered—you and me both.

It wasn't intentional, but as I wrote this book God showed me something. I realized much of the grief I went through, much of the hurt and heartbreak I experienced, came about simply because I held onto the secrets. I held onto them past their use-by date.

Actually, I'm not sure whether secrets ever have a use-by date. They are expired from the start.

If I had exposed the dark in *my* life to *His* light sooner, I'm convinced there could have been healing a lot faster. If I had listened to that "the truth will set you free" whisper earlier, guess what? I could've been freer, earlier—gotta love hindsight.

> I'm not sure whether secrets ever have a use-by date. They are expired from the start.

Truth and . . . Shopping?

You know those shopping channels? The ones you usually flick through when trying to get to your favorite show? I have another confession: *I love them.* I am a marketer's dream. It only takes thirty seconds for me to be convinced that I need a vacuum that can pick up a bowling ball. It only takes one minute to decide my life is not complete without that knife that can cut through a can. I have even gone so far as to pick up the phone and order Perfect Fit Buttons after watching the advertisement for them—they'll add to or subtract an inch from any waistband in seconds!

I know, it's sad . . . but at least I had enough self-control to withstand the world phenomena that was the Snuggie!

So what's my point? First, please, if you ever catch me watching the shopping channel, change the station! Second, the truth is we live in a world of spin and hype. Everything seems to have a bias, an agenda, or a convincing argument. We can turn any situation or piece of information into whatever we want with the right filter and caption.

In a world that's only interested in our "show reel" and fame, the Enemy tries to convince us we should only put our best foot forward, that our secrets should stay secret.

Here's my problem with that—if we keep our secrets in the dark (and you know the kind of secrets I'm talking about), we are wearing a mask. And although the mask might make us feel protected, it also shields us from receiving the love of God and the love of others.

It's time to take off our masks. It's time to confess who we really are.

I wonder what would happen if we decided, as friends (because we are friends now), that the Enemy is done convincing us our "secrets" are a good thing. I wonder what would happen if we decided we would finally begin to share our shame and weakness with those in our life who are trustworthy.

What would happen if we allowed those people to stand with us, encourage us, and pray us *through* those secrets? What if we weren't defined by those secrets? What if we could overcome them? Would we suddenly have the courage to stand with, encourage, and pray for those around us—just like they had done for us?

I think it's fairly safe to say it would prepare us to see a work of God that no one has ever seen. You know why? Because God never wasted a prepared man or woman. And this would be a surefire way to prepare ourselves. To do this requires humility and a willingness to be open, and that can be scary.

God never wasted a prepared man or woman.

But there is good news. Throughout the gospels, Jesus always drew close to those who humbled themselves and came close to Him. He healed the woman who touched Him although she was unclean. He healed the man who held out his withered hand and the paralyzed man whose friends lowered him into the house where Jesus was teaching.

Whether spiritual, emotional, or physical, Jesus healed them all. Why? Because He is near to the broken hearted (Proverbs 34:18).

Jesus sat down with the woman accused of adultery and, in her moment of exposure, covered her with grace. You can read that story in John 8:1-11. It's one of my absolute favorites. Jesus called a cheater and liar out of the tree where he was hiding. You can find that one in Luke 19:1-10. In Luke 23, Jesus hung on a tree while a thief who repented as he died hung next to Him. In his moment of physical death, Jesus promised the thief eternal life.

Jesus will cover *you* with grace if you will set aside your mask and be brave enough to stretch out your withered hand to Him. Watch as He heals you and makes you new again.

Believing Our Own Lies

My big brother is a pretty smart guy. No, I take that back. My big brother is a *very* smart guy. I may or may not have referred (significantly) to his essays to help me get through high school! It's okay. I came clean on that one, too. Don't judge. Even when my brother was in second grade, he was a triple threat—he was smart, he was cute, and he could rock the mullet hairstyle like nobody's business.

One day during class his teacher said to him, "You could do anything at all, Ryan. Why, you could even be prime minister!" I'm pretty sure his teacher didn't think much of it, but to Ryan, a seven-year-old kid who was dreaming about his future, this changed his life. My brother took this teacher's words to heart and, as a child, believed them wholeheartedly.

His teacher had said he could be anything he wanted, so why not?

Ryan went on to become captain of our primary school because that was the closest thing he could think of to being prime minister at his age. He wrote to the prime minister of Australia asking his advice on taking his job one day. I remember the day the reply came in the mail. It may as well have been from the queen (except not really, because Ryan's teacher didn't say he could be the queen one day . . . that would have been weird).

Anyway, the prime minister congratulated Ryan for his ambition and suggested he go to law school among other things. Guess what my brother is doing these days? He's a lawyer. (Unfortunately he no longer has his rockin' mullet.)

Because of the positive words of one teacher, a little boy was inspired to change the world. I don't know what my brother will end up doing, or whether he'll go into politics one day, but I do know he will change the world. How do I know? He acknowledges that he can do anything. His teacher said he could do anything, so why not?

Unfortunately, our lies have power, too. As long as you keep them secret . . . as long as you stay quiet and ashamed . . . as long as you believe the secrets you are keeping about yourself . . . they will control your destiny. The only way to take away their power is to confess them.

There is power in our confession.

If your world were transformed right now into what you confess over yourself, what would it look like?

If what you saw in the mirror morphed into what you confess about yourself, what would you look like?

If the relationships around you were only as close and deep as what you have confessed about them, what kind of friends would you have? If your education was based on your confession of how intelligent and smart you are, how would you be doing in class?

Scary questions, I know. But this is basically what Hebrews 11:3 says. We frame our world with our words.

Words are powerful. Secrets are powerful. Confessions are even *more* powerful.

It's time to start finding out what God says about you. Just like Ryan with his teacher, maybe it's time you started taking to heart what God says about you.

You can do anything you want; you could even be prime minister. He said so, so why not?

One Last Confession

I have another confession. Last one, I promise. I didn't want to sit down and write this last chapter. There's such a big part of me that doesn't want this journey to be over. It's like walking out of high school on your final day, getting home, and realizing there's no more studying left. And while part of you loves the idea of being able to sit down and lose yourself in the land of Pinterest or search sneezing pandas on YouTube, there's an amount of nostalgia and sadness.

A chapter of my life is coming to an end.

The truth is, I don't want it to be over. I've had so much fun writing my confessions and stories for you. And I've found freedom through it. At the start of this book (which feels like forever ago) I said I wanted to go on a personal journey of healing and maturity, and I feel like I have. I pray the same thing has happened for you.

I pray you were able to mix my words with the whispers of God. I hope somewhere along the way you found yourself in some of the stories I told, some of the Scriptures I recalled, and some of the lessons I learned. I pray that, somewhere along the way, He showed you that He is your home.

Above all else, I hope that along that way, He spoke to you.

Thank you for letting me be me, quirks and all. Thank you for letting me be honest and vulnerable. My prayer is that you will go and do the same.

Every honest confession is a good confession.

He is waiting for you.

So what are you waiting for?

Open Your Journal

I used to hate reading these kinds of books where the author challenged me to tell someone, to confess. I used to think, *Shut up, you don't know my situation!* Sometimes I would even close the book. Maybe you're reading this today and thinking the same.

You're right. I don't know your situation. I don't know everything you're feeling or going through. But I *do* know that no matter what it is, there's a God who loves you, forgives you, and wants *you* to live in freedom.

If you are facing something right now, and you feel the God-whisper to bring it into light, please tell someone. Trust me. It's time to be free.

About the Author

Elyse Murphy is a writer, pastor, and international speaker. She is driven by her passion for Jesus, the local church, and knowing the lyrics to every Taylor Swift song. Elyse is ministering to people with her message of hope and grace founded in Jesus Christ.

Having grown up as a pastor's kid in Sydney, Australia, Elyse graduated from Hillsong Leadership College and has been a pastor working with young people and young leaders ever since. She has ministered globally in both church and secular settings, inspiring people in their lives and challenging them in their faith.

Elyse now resides in Los Angeles, working with young adults and ministering as one of the pastors at Oasis Church in downtown Hollywood.

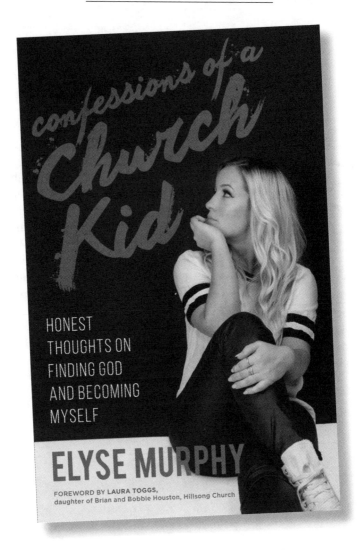

For more information about this and other valuable resources,
visit www.salubrisresources.com.